50 WALKS IN
Yorkshire Dales

50 WALKS OF 2–10 MILES

First published 2002
Researched and written by
David Winpenny, Sheila Bowker
and John Morrison
Field checked and updated 2009
by Jon Sparks
Reprinted February 2010

Commissioning Editor: Sandy Draper
Senior Editors: Penny Fowler
and David Popey
Designer: Tracey Butler
Picture Research: Liz Stacey
Proofreader: Jennifer Wood
Cartography provided by the Mapping
Services Department of AA Publishing

Produced by AA Publishing
© AA Media Limited 2010

We have taken all reasonable steps to
ensure that these walks are safe and
achievable by walkers with a realistic level
of fitness. However, all outdoor activities
involve a degree of risk and the publishers
accept no responsibility for any injuries
caused to readers whilst following these
walks. For more advice on walking safely
see page 176. The mileage range shown
on the front cover is for guidance only –
some walks may be less than or exceed
these distances.

Visit AA Publishing at theAA.com/shop

Cover reproduction by Keenes
Group, Andover
Printed by Printer Trento Srl, Italy

Acknowledgements
The Automobile Association would like
to thank the following photographers,
companies and picture libraries for their
assistance in the preparation of this book.

Abbreviations for the picture credits are as
follows: (t) top; (b) bottom; (l) left; (r) right;
(c) centre; (AA) AA World Travel Library.

3 AA/T Mackie; 7 AA/T Mackie; 11 AA/T
Mackie; 24/5 AA/T Mackie; 56/7 AA/D Tarn;
70 AA/T Mackie; 76/7 AA/J Morrison; 84/5
AA/D Tarn; 90/1 AA/D Tarn; 110 AA/T
Mackie; 126/7 AA/T Mackie.

Illustrations by Andrew Hutchinson

Every effort has been made to trace the
copyright holders, and we apologise in
advance for any accidental errors. We
would be happy to apply any corrections in
the following edition of this publication.

A04395

ISBN: 978-0-7495-6299-1
ISBN: 978-0-7495-6331-8

A CIP catalogue record for this book
is available from the British Library.

Right: View over West Burton, Wensleydale (Walk 11)

50 WALKS IN

Yorkshire Dales

50 WALKS OF 2–10 MILES

Contents

Contents

Rating

Each walk is rated for its relative difficulty compared to the other walks in this book. Walks marked +++ are likely to be shorter and easier with little total ascent. The hardest walks are marked +++ .

Walking in Safety

For advice and safety tips see page 176.

Locator Map

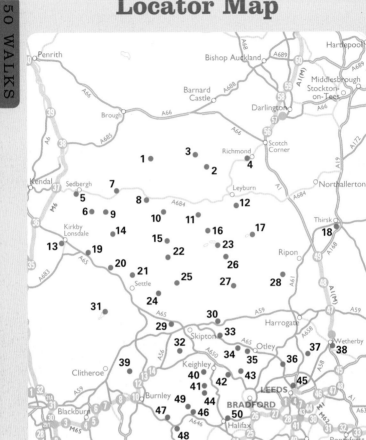

Legend

–→–	Walk Route		▦	Built-up Area
❶	Route Waypoint			Woodland Area
– – –	Adjoining Path		🏻	Toilet
|//	Viewpoint		P	Car Park
●	Place of Interest		🄰	Picnic Area
△	Steep Section		)(	Bridge

Right: A few houses scattered amongst the hills and countryside at Muker, Swaledale (Walk 1)

Introducing the Yorkshire Dales

The Yorkshire Dales are a series of beautiful valleys spreading out from the high Pennine watershed to the north of the industrial heartlands of West Yorkshire. For the most part they are protected by the Yorkshire Dales National Park, which covers an area of some 684 square miles (1773sq km) across the upland centre of northern England. Dominated by an underlying geology of gritstone and limestone, the Dales attract thousands of visitors every year, many of whom come simply for the joy of walking among the quiet meadows or on the bracing moors and fells.

Swaledale

In the north, Swaledale is the most peaceful and least developed of these great valleys. It was once a centre for lead mining and hand knitting, but now tourists bring most of its income, attracted by the simple remote villages such as Reeth, Keld and Muker, and the breathtaking contrasts of light and dark, between the meadows and the brooding hills. Richmond and its great castle stand guard over the entrance to the dale, where the River Swale spills out into the lowlands of the Plain of York. In the tributary valley of Arkengarthdale, the landscape is littered with the scars of lead mining, but the abandoned workings have gently tumbled back in to the landscape and now add a fascinating historical dimension to walks in this remote area.

Wensleydale

Next comes Wensleydale, famous for its crumbly cheese and its ceaseless array of waterfalls, of which Aysgarth and Hardraw are the highlights. Even in the upper dale, the scenery is less bleak than its northern neighbour, with larger villages like Bainbridge and Hawes serving as pretty urban honeypots. Over the watershed from here tumbles Dentdale, down to the cobbled village of Dent and the market town of Sedbergh. The map will tell you this is Cumbria, but the scenery is still very much Yorkshire Dales at heart.

PUBLIC TRANSPORT

Where the Dales run into Metropolitan West Yorkshire, you'll find the public transport network is superbly coordinated by Metro, the West Yorkshire Passenger Transport Executive. It is relatively cheap, trains and buses run well into the evening, there is through ticketing between operators and day passes are available. You can find out more from their website, www.wymetro.com, or call MetroLine on 0113 245 7676. In the more rural parts of the region and the Yorkshire Dales National Park, public transport is less plentiful and times may not be convenient for walking on the same day as travelling. However great strides have been made recently to improve the situation and there are now frequent buses in summer from the surrounding towns to the most popular walking areas. You can get timetable information on the internet at www.dalesbus. org. Arriva Northern operate passenger trains on the Settle-to-Carlisle line, which runs right across the middle of the area covered by this book. For more information call the national rail enquiry line on 08457 48 49 50, or check www.nationalrail.co.uk on the internet.

Ribblesdale

Still on the western side, Ingleton and Settle are the centres for exploring the limestone uplands that drain into the Ribble and Lune. You can be forgiven for straying into Lancashire here, perhaps to pick off the shapely summit of Pendle Hill or explore the fringes of the Forest of Bowland which lines the western side of Ribblesdale. Here, too, you'll find the famous Devil's Bridge at Kirkby Lonsdale, a soaring medieval structure over the River Lune, with the dark heights of Barbon Fell as a brooding backdrop.

Wharfedale

Returning to indisputable Yorkshire, Wharfedale, with its origins high on the fells at Oughtershaw, cuts a curving U-shaped line between craggy tops and limestone side valleys, past Hubberholme, Kettlewell and Grassington, then the romantic ruins of the priory at Bolton Abbey. From here the scenery changes subtly, the valley widening between heather moorlands through elegant Ilkley and, after one last moorland flourish on Otley's Chevin, beyond into the plains. From the ancient stone circle near the top of Ilkley's famous moor you can see for over 50 miles (80km), perhaps picking out the Kilburn White Horse on the North York Moors or the tower of York Minster on a clear day.

Nidderdale

Beside the Wharfe runs Nidderdale, a quiet, unassuming valley with great reservoirs in its upper reaches. Left out of the Yorkshire Dales National Park, this tranquil corner of grouse moors, pastureland and scattered settlements is now protected by the Nidderdale Area of Outstanding Natural Beauty. Again the haunting remains of once flourishing lead mines punctuate the dramatic landscape, none more so than at Greenhow Hill, between Pateley Bridge and Grassington, where the history of the mines can be traced back to Roman times.

Airedale

Running parallel with the Wharfe glides the River Aire. Its source obscured by complex limestone cave systems around Malham Cove, it cuts through gentle glaciated countryside before finding its shape again on the fringes of West Yorkshire. Here it narrows and the distinctive dark stone has been shaped into countless mills and their attendant rows of workers' houses. Above them brood silent moors, where once the Brontë sisters found their inspiration. Most of the mills have long since ceased production and in Bingley and Haworth you will find charming mini-townscapes, where the industrial past blends into a picturesque present of tumbling becks and woods bedecked with bluebells in the spring. You'll also catch a glimpse of the great Leeds and Liverpool Canal, snaking its tortuous route between the great conurbations which lie either side of the Pennines.

Calderdale

Last of all these dales comes Calderdale, winding down from the bleak moors above Todmorden through villages and towns once dominated by textile mills, but now softened and healed by time. The sheltered little wooded cloughs that line the main valley were once full of industry, but now you can walk around the valley of the Hebden Water and forget how close you are to the heart of urban West Yorkshire.

Legacy

Across this landscape have strode giants, poets, great writers and storytellers. But it is usually the humdrum workers we have to thank for the exhilarating opportunities to explore the region on foot. Miners trod their paths up the gills and beneath the crags to find lead and coal. Drovers ushered their cattle and sheep down the dales and over the fellsides on their way to the lucrative markets further south. Strings of ponies carried freight over passes and simple bridges to keep more populous regions in salt and wool. Mill workers hurried down stepped and paved tracks to work their shifts in the mill. This is the real legacy of the Dales, and their best kept secret. This book picks out 50 of the best routes for the walker in the footsteps of the great and the humble. There is no better way to explore the Yorkshire Dales.

Using this book

Information Panels

An information panel for each walk shows its relative difficulty (see page 5), the distance and total amount of ascent. An indication of the gradients you will encounter is shown by the rating ▲ ▲ ▲ (no steep slopes) to ▲ ▲ ▲ (several very steep slopes).

Maps

There are 50 maps, covering the walks. Some walks have a suggested option in the same area. The information panel for these walks will tell you how much extra walking is involved. On short-cut suggestions the panel will tell you the total distance if you set out from the start of the main walk. Where an option returns to the same point on the main walk, just the distance of the loop is given. Where an option leaves the main walk at one point and returns to it at another, then the distance shown is for the whole walk. The minimum time suggested is for reasonably fit walkers and doesn't allow for stops. Each walk has a suggested map.

Start Points

The start of each walk is given as a six-figure grid reference prefixed by two letters indicating which 100km square of the National Grid it refers to. You'll find more information on grid references on most Ordnance Survey maps.

Dogs

We have tried to give dog owners useful advice about how dog friendly each walk is. Please respect other countryside users. Keep your dog under control, especially around livestock, and obey local bylaws and other dog control notices.

Car Parking

Many of the car parks suggested are public, but occasionally you may find you have to park on the roadside or in a lay-by. Please be considerate when you leave your car, ensuring that access roads or gates are not blocked and that other vehicles can pass safely.

Right: Ribblehead Viaduct, Yorkshire Dales National Park (Walk 14)

A Riverside Circuit High in the Dales

A classic walk in Upper Swaledale from Keld to Muker along Kisdon Side, and back by the river.

DISTANCE 6 miles (9.7km)	**MINIMUM TIME** 2hrs 30min

ASCENT/GRADIENT 820ft (250m) ▲▲▲   **LEVEL OF DIFFICULTY** +++

PATHS Field and riverside paths and tracks, 5 stiles

LANDSCAPE Hillside and valley, hay meadows, riverside and waterfalls

SUGGESTED MAP OS Explorer OL30 Yorkshire Dales – Northern & Central

START/FINISH Grid reference: NY 892012

DOG FRIENDLINESS Dogs on leads (there are lots of sheep)

PARKING Signed car park at west end of village near Park Lodge

PUBLIC TOILETS Keld and Muker

Keld – its name is the Old Norse word for a spring – is one of the most remote of the Dales villages. Set at the head of Swaledale, its cluster of grey cottages is a centre for some of the most spectacular walks in North Yorkshire. This walk follows, for part of its way, the traditional route by which the dead of the upper Dales were taken the long distance for burial in Grinton churchyard. Leaving the village, the walk takes the Pennine Way as it follows the sweep of the Swale on its way down to Muker. This is Kisdon Side, on the slopes of the conical hill known as Kisdon. It was formed at the end of the ice age; the Swale used to flow west of the hill but glacial debris blocked its course and forced it to the east, in its current bed.

Muker and the Mines

As the Pennine Way goes west, eventually to climb the slopes of Great Shunner Fell, the walk joins the Corpse Way and descends into Muker. It is worth taking some time to explore the village. Like many Swaledale settlements, it expanded in the 18th and 19th centuries because of local lead mining. The prominent Literary Institute was built for the mining community; though in a nice reverse of fortunes, when the new chapel came to be built in the 1930s, dressed stone taken from the ore hearths at the Old Gang Mine down the valley was used. The Anglican church, which eventually did away with the long journey to Grinton, dates from 1580.

Rocks and Crackpot

Beyond Muker, the walk passes through hay meadows and along the banks of the Swale. Both sandstone and limestone are found in this section; look out for the sandstone bed underlying the river. The limestone of the area is part of the thick Ten Fathom bed, one of the Yoredale series of sedimentary rocks. Where the valley of Swinner Gill crosses the path are the remains of a small smelt mill which served the nearby Beldi Hill and Swinner Gill Mines. As you ascend the hill beyond, the ruins of Crackpot Hall, a farmhouse long abandoned because of mining subsidence and changes in farming fortune, are to your right.

KELD

As the track descends the valley side, the waterfall of Kisdon Force is below you on the Swale, and there are high overhanging crags on the opposite bank. Further along, you turn downhill to the footbridge over the river, passing East Gill Force. Like all the Dales falls, the volume of its water can vary wildly from the merest summer trickle to a raging winter torrent. Whatever its condition, the rocks around can be very slippery and you should take special care if you leave the path to get a better view.

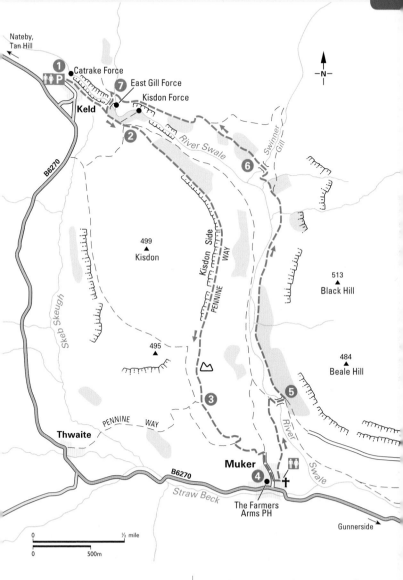

WALK 1 DIRECTIONS

1 Walk back down the car park entrance road, and straight ahead down a gravel track, signed 'Muker'. Continue along at the upper level, ignoring a path downhill to the left. Go through a gate, pass a sign to Kisdon Upper Force, and continue along the path below crags to a signpost.

② Turn right, following the Pennine Way, and go up to a gap in a wall and another signpost. Go left and follow a rough but mostly level path along Kisdon Side, first above woodland then across more open slopes. Cross a ladder stile as the path starts to descend. Go down to a signpost and bear right to another signpost, where the Pennine Way goes right.

③ Bear left down a walled track, marked 'Muker'. The track becomes gravelled and then metalled, finally descending into a walled lane on the edge of the village. Continue to a T-junction.

④ Turn left and in a few paces left again by a sign to Gunnerside and Keld. Follow the paved path through six gates to the river. Turn sharp right and walk downstream to a footbridge.

⑤ Ascend steps beyond the footbridge and turn left, signed 'Keld'. Follow a clear track up along the valley, until it curves right into Swinner Gill. Cross a footbridge by the remains of lead workings, and go up to a wooden gate.

⑥ Go straight ahead up the hill and through woodland. The track levels out, then starts to descend, winding left round a barn then swinging back right. Continue steadily downhill to reach a gate above East Gill Force.

⑦ Fork left by a wooden seat, at a sign to Keld. Follow the path down to a footbridge then bear right, uphill, to a T-junction, where you turn right and follow the track back to the car.

Around Reeth in the Heart of Swaledale

Farmers, miners, knitters and nuns all played their part in the history of this part of Swaledale.

DISTANCE 5.5 miles (8.8km)   MINIMUM TIME 2hrs

ASCENT/GRADIENT 508ft (155m) ▲▲▲   LEVEL OF DIFFICULTY +++

PATHS Field and riverside paths, lanes and woodland, 14 stiles

LANDSCAPE Junction of Swaledale and Arkengarthdale, with field and surrounding moorland

SUGGESTED MAP OS Explorer OL30 Yorkshire Dales – Northern & Central

START/FINISH Grid reference: SE 039993

DOG FRIENDLINESS Dogs should be on leads for majority of walk

PARKING In Reeth, behind fire station, or by the Green (voluntary payment requested)

PUBLIC TOILETS Reeth, near Buck Hotel

Reeth has always had a strategic role in the Yorkshire Dales. Set above the junction of Swaledale and Arkengarthdale on Mount Calva, it controlled the important route westwards from Richmond. Sheep were, for a long time, the basis of Reeth's prosperity – it has been a market town since 1695 – and there are still annual sheep sales each autumn, as well as the important Reeth Show around the beginning of September. The wool was used in Reeth's important knitting industry– both the men and women would click away with their needles at stockings and other garments. Reeth also used to be a centre for the lead mining industry, which extended up Arkengarthdale and over Marrick Moor.

Two Bridges and a Church

Reeth Bridge, reached by the Leyburn road from the Green, has suffered over the years from the effects of the swollen River Swale. The present bridge dates from the early 18th century, replacing one washed away in 1701, itself built after its predecessor succumbed in 1547. The path beside the river takes us to Grinton Bridge. Nearby is Grinton church, once the centre of a huge parish that took in the whole of Swaledale, making very long journeys necessary for marriages and funerals. Curiously, it began life as a mission church for the Augustinian Canons of far-away Bridlington Priory on the east coast.

Nuns and Schools at Marrick

The approach to Marrick Priory along the lane suggests that you are about to reach one of the most important churches in the Dales. In a way that is true. Marrick in the Middle Ages was home to a group of Benedictine Nuns. It was founded by Roger de Aske, whose descendent, Robert, was one of the leaders of the Pilgrimage of Grace, the uprising against King Henry VIII's closure of the monasteries. Hilda Prescott's novel *The Man on a Donkey*, about Robert Aske and the Pilgrimage, is partly set at Marrick.

REETH

Today the nuns' buildings are partly demolished or absorbed into farm buildings. The church was reduced in size in 1811, and the complex is now used as a Youth Centre for the Diocese of Ripon and Leeds, offering outdoor sports and adventure training.

After Marrick Priory the path climbs steeply uphill on rough stone steps called the Nun's Causey (a corruption of causeway). Now used as part of the Coast to Coast Walk, from St Bee's Head in Cumbria to Robin Hood's Bay on the east coast, this is said to be the route which the nuns from the Priory built so they could reach the old Richmond road that ran along the summit of the hill. The original 365 steps have been broken up and removed over the centuries, but the path still retains a suitably medieval atmosphere.

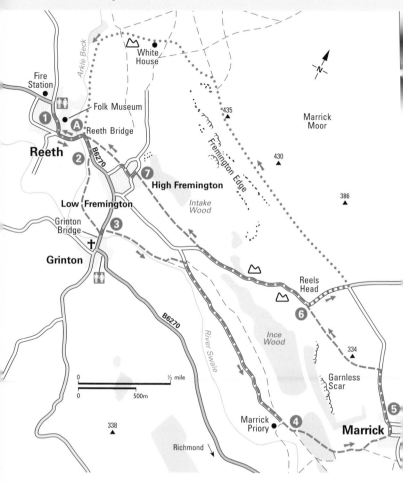

WALK 2 DIRECTIONS

❶ From the Green, walk downhill, in the direction of Leyburn, to Reeth Bridge. Over the bridge, continue along the

road as it swings right. About 100yds (91m) along, turn right at a footpath sign to Grinton.

❷ Follow the riverside path to a signpost, then continue on a well-

REETH

marked path across fields to ascend steps on to Grinton Bridge. Turn left a few paces, cross the road and take a track beside the bridge.

3 Follow the riverside path for about 0.5 mile (800m) to a metalled lane. Turn right and follow the lane to Marrick Priory. Walk past the buildings, over a cattle grid, and bear left through a gate signed 'Marrick'.

4 Walk up the grassy track, then follow the paved path through woodland. Continue through fields, with a wall on the right, into a metalled lane. Opposite Harlands House turn left, then left again at a triangular junction.

5 Follow the road for 0.25 mile (400m), and turn left over a stile at a footpath sign. Follow the wall, and cross it a waymarked stile. Continue along the wall then keep on in the same direction, descending slightly to meet a road.

6 Turn left and follow the road for 0.75 mile (1.2km). On a left bend near an obvious track to a farm, cross a stile on the right, signed 'Fremington'. Go straight ahead to a stile then continue along the well-marked path through fields, until a final gate leads onto a walled path behind houses. Go straight ahead to a lane.

7 Turn left then first right. As the lane bends left, go ahead to a stile by a gate. Keep by the wall on the left, and follow the path through more stiles back to Reeth Bridge. Cross the bridge and follow the road back to the Green.

EXTENDING THE WALK
You can extend the walk from Point **6** by turning right, uphill, then left through a stile by the road sign to Marrick. Cross a field, follow a wall on the left, then keep on the track over Fremington Edge. Descend past spoil heaps, go through a gate and follow a faint path half right. Bear right along the brink of a very steep slope (beware broken crags below), then slant down to a gap in a wall. Continue the slanting descent through the remains of chert mines. Reach a track near a footpath sign, follow a grassy path above White House to a gated stile, bear left on a green path and descend steeply to a track, signpost and stile. Cross the stile, walk past a barn and through two more stiles, then bear left, parallel with the river, with a wall on your left. Go through a stile, pass a barn, then through the left of two gates in a crossing wall. Continue through a long narrow field to the road by Reeth Bridge, rejoining the main walk.

Leaden Arkengarthdale

Around an austere valley where hundreds of lead workers once toiled.

DISTANCE *8 miles (12.9km)*	MINIMUM TIME *3hrs 15min*		

ASCENT/GRADIENT *1,213ft (370m)* ▲▲▲ LEVEL OF DIFFICULTY +++

PATHS *Mostly clear tracks, some heather moor, 4 stiles*

LANDSCAPE *Mining-scarred moorland, with evocative remains of industry*

SUGGESTED MAP *OS Explorer OL30 Yorkshire Dales – Northern & Central*

START/FINISH *Grid reference: NZ 005024*

DOG FRIENDLINESS *Off lead for much of walk, except where sheep are present*

PARKING *Pay-and-display car park at south end of Langthwaite village*

PUBLIC TOILETS *None en route*

The quiet villages of Arkle Town and Langthwaite are grey clusters of houses in the austere splendour of Arkengarthdale. One of the most northerly of the valleys in the Dales, it runs northwards from Swaledale into dark moorland, with the battle-scarred Stainmore beyond its head. This isolation and stillness is deceptive, however, for until the beginning of the 20th century the surrounding hills were mined for lead. The metal was first dug here in prehistoric times, but industrial mining of the great veins of lead really began in the 17th century. By 1628 there was a smelt mill beside the Slei Gill, which you will pass on the walk, and it is possible to pick out the evidence of some of the early miners' methods.

Booze and Gunpowder

Booze (Norse for 'the house on the curved hillside') is now just a cluster of farm buildings, but was once a thriving mining community with more than 40 houses. Between Booze and Slei Gill you will pass the arched entrance to a level (a miners' tunnel) and behind it the remains of Tanner Rake Hush. This desolate valley is full of tumbled rock, left behind when the dammed stream at the top of the valley was allowed to rush down, exposing the lead veins. You'll pass the spoil heaps of Windegg Mines, before returning to the valley near Scar House, now a shooting lodge owned by the Duke of Norfolk but once belonging to the mine master. Near Eskeleth Bridge is the powder house, a small octagonal building, set safely by itself in a field. Built about 1804, it served the Octagon Smelt Mill, the remains of which can be traced near by. Just after you turn right along the road are the ruins of Langthwaite Smelt Mill. Lord of the Manor Charles Bathurst held the mining rights here for much of the 18th century. The CB Inn near the road junction is really the Charles Bathurst, in his honour.

Mining the west of the valley was more difficult than on the eastern side. This was an area known in the 19th century as the Hungry Hushes – the lead mined here was scarce and hard-won. The miners' tracks ascend the hill and eventually pass the junction of two long chimney flues. The

ARKENGARTHDALE

walk then returns via Turf Moor into Langthwaite – it needs a feat of the imagination to visualise its heyday, with a tight-knit community of hardened miners and their families.

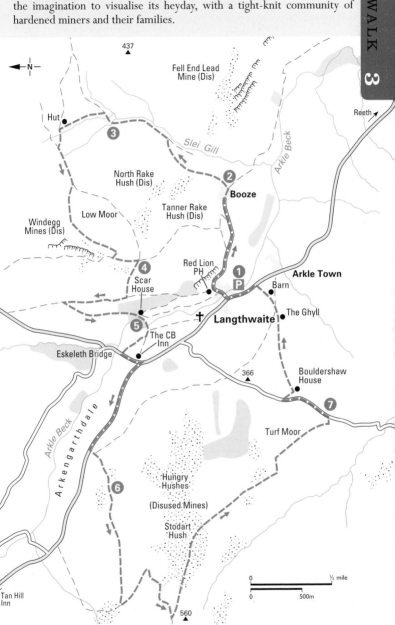

WALK 3 DIRECTIONS

❶ Leave the car park, turn right, then right over the bridge into Langthwaite. Climb the narrow lane between cottages. The lane becomes a track. Ignore two left forks and continue to the hamlet of Booze. Go straight through the yard of Town Farm and follow a rutted track up and left to a gate.

ARKENGARTHDALE

2 Continue ahead on a green track slanting down through spoil heaps and past ruined Sleigill House to the stream. Walk up the valley, go through a gate and cross the stream near a limekiln.

3 Climb the steep bank, go through new tree-plantings and follow green paths through the heather. Pass a wooden hut and turn left on a broad track. Follow the main track through a slight valley, then bearing left over the moor and down to a T-junction with a wall just below. Where this falls back, go down right to a gate in the corner.

4 Follow the small gully downhill and past waymarks to a level track. Turn right and follow the track, traversing the hillside until it bends sharp left to meet a stony track. Turn left to a house then bear right, through the garden and down a slanting green track, eventually entering woodland.

5 Emerge alongside Scar House. Follow the drive downhill and over a bridge. Bear right on a walled track,

then turn right through gateposts and walk to a road. Turn left, uphill, to a T-junction. Turn right and follow the road for 0.5 mile (800m). Opposite a barn, turn left on an obvious track.

6 Turn right at the far side of a gravelled area, cross a grassy area and slant uphill towards a prominent flat-topped spoil heap. Just before this, the track bends sharp left then winds uphill to reach a T-junction near the crest. Turn left and follow the clear track, along the ridge then bearing right down to a road.

7 Turn left. Pass above a farm (Bouldershaw), then turn right at a bridleway sign. Turn left just before the farmyard and go straight down a green track. At The Ghyll, join its access track but as it bends right bear left and down to a stile in the bottom right corner of the field. Go down to the road. Turn left back to the car park.

Richmond's Drummer Boy

Following in the steps of the
Richmond Drummer, to Easby Abbey.

DISTANCE 6 miles (9.7km)   MINIMUM TIME 2hrs 20min

ASCENT/GRADIENT 656ft (200m) ▲▲▲   LEVEL OF DIFFICULTY ✦✦✦

PATHS Field and riverside paths, a little town walking, 15 stiles

LANDSCAPE Valley of River Swale and its steep banks

SUGGESTED MAP OS Explorer 304 Darlington & Richmond

START/FINISH Grid reference: NZ 168012

DOG FRIENDLINESS Dogs should be on leads for most of walk

PARKING Friars Close long-stay car park

PUBLIC TOILETS Friars Close car park, Richmond Town Centre and Round Howe car park

The first part of the walk follows much of the route taken by the legendary Richmond Drummer Boy. At the end of the 18th century, the story says, soldiers in Richmond Castle discovered a tunnel that was thought to lead from there to Easby Abbey. They sent their drummer boy down it, beating his drum so they could follow from above ground. His route went under the Market Square and along to Frenchgate, then beside the river towards the abbey. At the spot now marked by the Drummer Boy Stone, the drumming stopped. The Drummer Boy was never seen again. The Green Howards Regimental Museum in the Market Square can tell you more about the drummer boy and his regiment.

Abbey and Church

Easby Abbey, whose remains are seen on your walk, was founded for Premonstratensian Canons in 1155 by the Constable of Richmond Castle. Although not much of the church remains, some of the other buildings survive well, including the gatehouse, built about 1300. The refectory is also impressive, and you can see the infirmary, the chapter house and the dormitory. Just by the abbey ruins is the parish church, St Agatha's. It contains a replica of the Anglo-Saxon Easby Cross (the original is in the British Museum) and a set of medieval wall paintings showing Old Testament scenes of Adam and Eve, on the north wall, and the life of Jesus on the south, as well as depictions of activities such as pruning and hawking.

After the Abbey, you'll cross the River Swale on the old railway bridge, and follow the track bed. This was part of the branch line from Richmond to Darlington, which opened in 1846. It was closed in 1970. The station has been restored as a cinema and shopping centre, with a café. Look right over Richmond Bridge after you have passed below the castle to see how the stonework differs from one end to the other. It was built by different contractors, one working for Richmond Council and one for the North Riding of Yorkshire. In the hillside below Billy Bank Wood, which you enter beyond the bridge, were copper mines dating back to the 15th century.

RICHMOND

After you have climbed the hill and crossed the 12 stiles (between Points **5** and **6**), you're following the old route of the Swale, which thousands of years ago changed its course and formed the hill known as Round Howe.

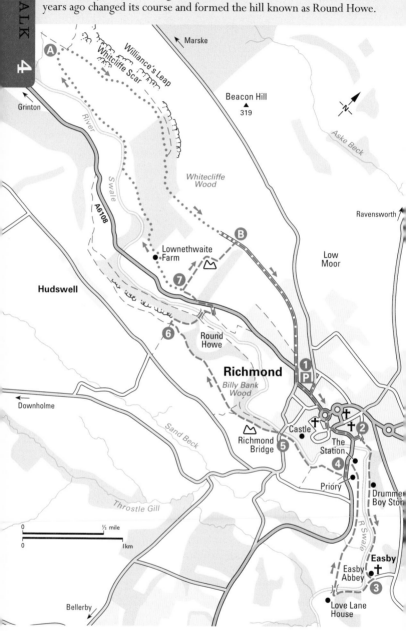

WALK 4 DIRECTIONS

1 Leave the Friars Close car park and turn right, then left at the T-junction. At the roundabout,

go straight on, down Ryder's Wynd. At the bottom turn left, then go right into Station Road. Just past the church, take Lombards Wynd left.

2 Turn right at the next junction and follow the track, passing to the right of the Drummer Boy Stone, along the path to a gate. Bear right after the gate, still parallel with the river, bearing right again to a gate then along beside the Abbey in the village of Easby.

3 Just beyond the car park turn right, along the track. Follow the wall on the left to Love Lane House. Turn right over the old railway bridge. Follow the track bed, crossing a metalled lane, to the station. Go to the left of the station building to the road.

4 Turn left, up the road, then turn right up Priory Villas, bearing right to go in front of the houses. Go through three waymarked gates, keeping parallel to the river. Cross some playing fields and pass a clubhouse to a road.

5 Cross the road and take a signed path opposite, to the left of the cottage. Climb steeply through the woodland, through a gate and straight on to a stile. At the end of the woodland, bend right, then left to pass a stile in a former crossing fence. Follow the signed path over 12 more stiles. After the

last, bear right over another stile, turn left to follow the wall, then go over another stile.

6 Turn right to go through a gate. Follow the track as it bends downhill, through a gate, to a bridge. Cross it and walk to the lane. Go left and left again at the main road. After 200yds (183m), go right up a bridleway-signed track, to a junction.

7 Turn right and follow the track uphill, bearing right, then left near the farmhouse, to reach a metalled lane. Turn right and follow the lane back into Richmond. Go ahead at the main road and follow it as it bends left to the garage, where you turn left back to the car park.

EXTENDING THE WALK
You can extend this walk by continuing up the banks of the River Swale, along the tracks from Point **7**, as far as Point **A**. Return beneath the crags of Whitcliffe Scar to rejoin the main route at Point **B**.

Overleaf: Wispy clouds over a bridge and castle tower in Richmond (Walk 4)

Sedbergh and the Quakers

*A gentle walk from Sedbergh
to the Quaker hamlet of Brigflatts.*

DISTANCE 4.5 miles (7.2km)   **MINIMUM TIME** 1hr 30min

ASCENT/GRADIENT 131ft (40m) ▲▲▲   **LEVEL OF DIFFICULTY** ✦✦✦

PATHS Mostly on field and riverside paths, 7 stiles

LANDSCAPE Playing fields give way to rich farmland, dominated by fells

SUGGESTED MAP OS Explorer OL19 Howgill Fells & Upper Eden Valley

START/FINISH Grid reference: SD 659921

DOG FRIENDLINESS Keep dogs on lead when animals in fields

PARKING Pay-and-display car park just off Sedbergh main street (which is one-way, from west)

PUBLIC TOILETS By car park

The solid, stone-built town of Sedbergh, one of the largest settlements in the Yorkshire Dales National Park, was once in the West Riding of Yorkshire, but has been part of Cumbria since 1974. Two things – the Howgill Fells, especially the southernmost peaks of Winder and Crook, and Sedbergh School, which wraps itself around much of the town's south side – dominate this friendly town. Among its most notable old boys are the geologist Adam Sedgwick (see Walk 6) and the international rugby player Will Carling. Brilliant mathematician John Dawson taught Sedgwick and a group of other gifted scholars at the school in the late 18th century, and is commemorated with a bust by the sculptor Flaxman, high on the south nave wall in Sedbergh parish church. Almost opposite the church is the school's oldest building, built in 1716, now the school library.

The Quaker Link

The Sedbergh area is noted for its Quaker associations. In 1652 the founder of the Society of Friends, George Fox, came to the town and preached from a bench beneath a yew tree in the churchyard to a great crowd of people attending the Hiring Fair. On Firbank Fell, north west of Sedbergh, Fox again preached to a large crowd, this time from a large stone, still known as Fox's Pulpit. This meeting is said to mark the inception of the Society of Friends. Fox wrote: 'This was the place that I had seen a people coming forth in white raiment; and a mighty meeting there was and it is to this day near Sedbergh which I gathered in the name of Jesus.'

Meeting at Brigflatts

The best reminder of the early days of the Quakers in the area is to be found in the tiny hamlet of Brigflatts. Fox stayed here with Richard Robinson in a farmhouse in 1652, and in 1674 the Friends of the district decided to build a Meeting House. It still survives, and is the oldest in the North and the third oldest in England. From the outside, it looks like a typical whitewashed cottage of the period, though, unlike most cottages,

SEDBERGH

it had a stone roof from the start. Each winter the cracks in the slate were stuffed with moss to stop the rain getting in. George Fox was there in 1677, noting 'a great concourse…there were about 500/600 persons present. A very good meeting it was.' Around the beginning of the 18th century a schoolroom was built over the stable and the gallery was put up to accommodate the large gatherings. At the foot of the gallery stairs look out for the dog pen that was provided for the sheepdogs accompanying their masters to the meetings. Just up the lane from the Meeting House is the small and peaceful Burial Ground, first used in 1656.

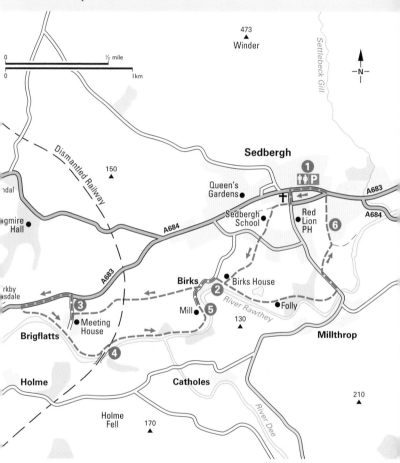

WALK 5 DIRECTIONS

❶ From the car park, turn right along the main street. At the junction with the main road turn left. At the churchyard, turn right, signed 'Cattle Market or Busk Lane'. At the next signpost, go left behind the pavilion, then straight ahead through two kissing gates to a road. Cross and go down a track beside playing fields. Go through a kissing gate near a barn and follow a green path to pass Birks House.

❷ Go through a kissing gate to a lane and turn left. Pass several houses then go right, through a metal kissing gate, and bear half left to a waymarker, roughly

WALK 5

following the Brigflatts sign. Follow the wall and then cross a field to a small bridge under the old railway. Drop down and bear slightly left on a path across fields to a gate onto a quiet lane opposite the Quaker Burial Ground.

3 Turn left to visit the Meeting House, then return to the gate, continuing on up the lane to the main road. Turn left. Just beyond the bend sign, go through a signed metal kissing gate in the hedge on the left. Follow the narrow path to meet the River Rawthey and walk upstream to a large railway bridge.

4 Go through the gate and slant up the embankment. Cross and descend back to the river. Continue along the riverside, passing the confluence of the Rawthey and the Dee, and reach a tarmac lane by an old mill.

5 Follow the lane back into Birks. Go right, though the kissing gate signed 'Rawthey Way' (you went through this the other way earlier in the walk). By the hedge around Birks House, bear right and down towards the river. Walk alongside another playing field to a stile. Climb slightly left to go past a folly. Follow the left side of a wood, then enter at a kissing gate. At a footpath sign, bear right down a sunken path. Leave the wood and follow a clear path across

a field to emerge on to a road by a bridge. Turn left. By the 'Sedbergh' sign, go right, though a stile. Cross the field to another stile, then bear left alongside a wall to another kissing gate.

WHERE TO EAT AND DRINK

The Bull, the Dalesman and the Red Lion all offer pub meals at lunchtime and evenings (not Mondays at the Red Lion). The Sedbergh Café on the main street welcomes walkers, while Ellie's Bakery & Tearooms is good for vegetarians.

6 Cross a drive, go downhill and straight on along a lane to the main road. Cross the road then turn left at the 'No Entry' sign, along Sedbergh's main street to the car park.

WHILE YOU'RE THERE

Spend a few quiet minutes in Queen's Gardens in Sedbergh. Described as 'a forgotten Victorian Park', the gardens are west of the town centre, just off the Kendal road. Presented to Sedbergh in 1906 by the splendidly named Mrs Upton-Cottrell-Dormer of Ingmire Hall in memory of Queen Victoria, there are shady trees and specially created glades for wildlife.

WHAT TO LOOK FOR

The Howgill Fells, very different from the rest of the Yorkshire Dales, are huge, rounded humps of hills that seem to crowd in on each other like elephants at a watering hole. They are formed from pinkish sandstone and slates, 100 million years older than the limestone that underlies much of the rest of the National Park. The hills have few of the stone walls you will see elsewhere in the Dales – they are mostly common grazing land for the local farms and escaped the passion for enclosure in earlier centuries. One of the spectacular sights of the Dales, the great ribbon of waterfalls known as Cautley Spout is worth the drive from Sedbergh in the direction of Kirkby Stephen – park by the Cross Keys, a temperance inn. You can view the falls from there or walk part of the way towards them on a good path.

Adam Sedgwick's Inspirational Dent

From the birthplace of a geologist, through the countryside that inspired his work.

DISTANCE *6 miles (9.7km)* MINIMUM TIME *2hrs 30min*

ASCENT/GRADIENT *918ft (280m)* ▲▲▲ LEVEL OF DIFFICULTY ✦✦✦

PATHS *Tracks, field and riverside paths, some roads, 3 stiles*

LANDSCAPE *Moorland and farmland, with wide views of Dentdale*

SUGGESTED MAP *OS Explorer OL2 Yorkshire Dales – Southern & Western*

START/FINISH *Grid reference: SD 704871*

DOG FRIENDLINESS *On lead in farmland and for riverside sections*

PARKING *Pay-and-display car park at west end of Dent*

PUBLIC TOILETS *At car park*

Dentdale is sometimes called 'the hidden valley'. Unlike most of the Yorkshire Dales it looks west towards the Lake District, and at its western end the limestone landscape gives way suddenly to the rounded Howgill Fells. It seems to have a milder climate and it is more thickly wooded, too. Its 'capital', Dent, is one of the most individual villages of the Dales. Its dog-legged main street is lined with stone cottages that front directly on to the cobbles, or cluster around the church. It is a fascinating spot to explore, with the added benefit of good pubs and tea shops. It is also a busy place in the summer, with tourists and walkers attracted by the special feel of what comedian and walker Mike Harding has called 'the bonniest of all Dales villages'.

Man of the Rocks and the Terrible Knitters

Pride of place in the main street is a drinking fountain made from a huge boulder of Shap granite and simply inscribed 'Adam Sedgwick 1785–1873'. It is a bold and simple memorial to Dent's most famous son. Sedgwick was born in the Old Parsonage by the village green; he was the son of the parson, and the surgeon who delivered him was, perhaps prophetically, another Dentdale genius, mathematician John Dawson. Sedgwick went to Sedbergh School and on to Cambridge, where his study of geology, inspired by the rocks of Dentdale, made him among the foremost authorities on the subject. He eventually became Professor of Geology at Cambridge – the university's fascinating geology museum is now named after him. He returned regularly to Dent, where his brother and his nephew both succeeded his father as vicar. 'Whenever I have revisited the hills and dales of my native country,' he wrote in 1866, when he was 81, 'I have felt a new swell of emotion, and said to myself, here is the land of my birth; this was the home of my boyhood, and is still the home of my heart.'

As well as farming, the other great industry of Dent, well into the 19th century, was knitting. 'The Terrible Knitters of Dent', the poet Southey called them – intending a compliment on their speed and industry. Men, women and children all knitted – often while engaged at other work. Adam

DENT

Sedgwick remembered that 'with a speed that cheated the eye they went on with their respective tasks. Beautiful gloves were thrown off complete; and worsted stockings made good progress. There was no dreary noise of machinery; but there was the merry heart-cheering sound of the human tongue.' Dent's woollen socks kept the feet of the British Army warm while they fought Napoleon.

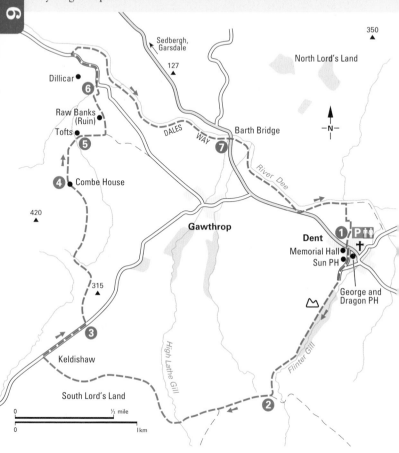

WALK 6 DIRECTIONS

❶ Leaving the car park, go up the lane almost opposite, left of the Memorial Hall. Pass the green and keep straight on at the 'Flinter Gill' signpost. The lane becomes a stony track climbing through trees alongside Flinter Gill. Slowly the gradient eases and the trees peter out. Finally you reach a gate beside a seat high on the fellside. Go through the gate to a T-junction of tracks.

❷ Turn right, signed 'Keldishaw'. Follow the walled track, eroded by 4x4 traffic, for 1.5 miles (2.4km), keeping straight ahead at the only junction. Reaching a tarmac road, turn right for 0.25 mile (400m) to the crest of a rise and a signpost on the left.

❸ Go through the gate and follow the grassy track past small shakeholes to a ladder stile. Continue along a dilapidated wall to reach a track. This trends right

DENT

below a slope scattered with trees, then contours round with great views of the valley, eventually descending through the yard of a recently restored farmhouse.

❹ Follow the access track winding down the hill, crossing a couple of tumbledown walls before marker posts on the left lead you away from the track. Meet a stream, go left along the bank for a few paces, then cross a simple bridge of two stones. Climb the bank beyond and go straight ahead through a farmyard.

❺ Continue down the farm track until it almost levels out alongside a line of trees. Turn sharp left by a large oak, through a waymarked gate. Walk diagonally down the field towards a ruined farmhouse smothered in elder trees. Pass to its right and continue down, soon joining a clearer track. Follow this downhill to reach a drive and go right a few paces to a lane.

❻ Turn left along the lane. Follow it round to the right, then back left as it levels out in the valley bottom. Watch for a ladder stile by a barn on the left. Don't use this, but look for a signpost on the right, about 50 paces further on, with a plank bridge and stile just below it. From the stile cross the field to the river bank. Go right, following the river (and the Dales Way) upstream for about 0.75 mile (1.2km) to reach stone steps leading to a squeeze stile onto a stone bridge.

❼ Go straight across the road and down more steps to continue along the riverside path, until it meets the road. Turn left; the path soon leaves the road again. Follow the riverbank through two more fields, then turn right on an obvious path. Go through two more fields; at the top of the second turn left, then go right on a track back into the car park.

Through Grisedale, 'The Dale that Died'

The derelict farmsteads of this once-thriving dale tell their story of hardship and surrender.

DISTANCE 5 miles (8km)   MINIMUM TIME 2hrs 15min

ASCENT/GRADIENT 590ft (180m) ▲▲▲   LEVEL OF DIFFICULTY ✦✦✦

PATHS Moorland paths and tracks, may be boggy, 16 stiles

LANDSCAPE Rough moors and hidden valleys, railway within earshot

SUGGESTED MAP OS Explorer OL19 Howgill Fells & Upper Eden Valley

START/FINISH Grid reference: SD 787918

DOG FRIENDLINESS Sheep on moorland – keep dogs under close control

PARKING Roadside parking on road to Garsdale Station

PUBLIC TOILETS None en route

Whenever Grisedale is mentioned, it is tagged 'The Dale that Died'. This perhaps unfortunate label was the title of a television documentary made in the mid-1970s that followed the fortunes, and misfortunes, of families farming in this remote valley that pushes north from Garsdale towards the massive heights of Wild Boar Fell. The programme in particular dealt with a former miner, Joe Gibson, who struggled against the climate, misfortune and the lack of subsidies for upland farmers to try to make even a bare living from the land – a struggle that eventually proved unequal and ended with his retreat from Grisedale. The fields that Joe and his neighbours once tended have now reverted to moorland and scrub, and a plantation of conifers climbs the side of East Baugh Fell from the valley bottom. Nearly all the farmhouses are now derelict. At the head of the valley stands Round Ing, once a substantial building with barns and animal sheds. Now it has tumbled down, its walls diminishing in height every year. What remains of the plants and shrubs in its garden still bloom in summer, but, like West Scale and East Scale a little downstream, it is a place of sadness and lost hope.

From the Pigs to the Railway

Grisedale's earlier history is obscure – perhaps unsurprisingly for such a remote place. Its name comes from Old Norse and means 'the valley in which the pigs were kept', so the dale must have been farmed from its earliest days. In the Middle Ages it was owned by the monks of Jervaulx Abbey at the far end of Wensleydale; Grisedale is only about a mile (1.6km) from the River Ure as it begins its decent though Wensleydale. Grisedale seems to have been populated steadily throughout the later centuries, partly because it was adjacent to one of the main routes to the Lake District from the east – Wordsworth recommends the route to Kendal through Wensleydale passing the foot of Grisedale. It also received a boost when the Settle-to-Carlisle railway arrived in 1876.

After Round Ing, the walk passes the derelict barns of Flust, where it fords a stream, then continues near the inhabited farmsteads of Fea

GRISEDALE

Fow and East House. It then crosses the ridge (and the county boundary between Cumbria and North Yorkshire) with views towards Ingleborough and Whernside, and descends through South Lunds Pasture to Grisedale Crossing on the Settle-to-Carlisle railway line. Beside a typical railway house is a metal footbridge across the line, put up in 1886 to replace an earlier wooden one. Here the line is just below its highest point, 1,169ft (356m), the Ais Gill summit.

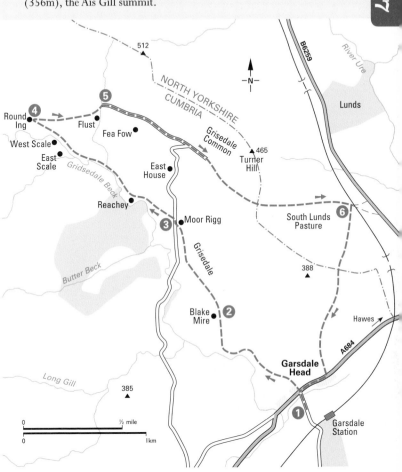

WALK 7 DIRECTIONS

❶ Walk down to the main road. Cross at the junction and take a stile signed 'Grisedale and Flust'. Follow a faint path just above the wall on the left, to find another stile in a wall. Follow the sign on a faint path across the moor to another signpost, then descend to another stile right of Bleak Mire farmhouse beyond the bend of the wall.

❷ Go half right, aiming slightly left of a barn to a gap in a crumbling wall. Continue straight ahead and descend to pass ruined buildings, then turn right, over a stile. Head towards a barn and another stile behind it. Continue to a signpost near a white-painted farmhouse.

❸ Cross the lane to another signpost, then down to another stile. From this, bear left near the

33

WALK 7

wall, then descend to follow the beck. Go through a gate and, near the restored house at Reachey, bear right, following waymarks, to a signposted stile. Follow the beck upstream to a packhorse bridge near deserted East Scale. Do not cross the bridge, but climb by a ruined wall to a gap and fallen signpost. Follow sheep tracks across the moor, aiming for an isolated tree which marks the ruins of Round Ing.

4 At Round Ing double back right, over rising ground to a waymarked post by the corner of a wall. Continue towards the right end of a plantation on the hillside. Go through two gates left of the barn at Flust to join a good track.

5 Follow the track to the junction with a rough metalled lane. Continue ahead on a greener track. This fades, but keep straight ahead over level moorland to a prominent stile on the left and descend the rush-covered, pathless slope beyond. When the

slope steepens, aim for the grey footbridge over the railway.

6 Go over a stile beside the railway, pass the footbridge and then cross a stile in a corner close to the line. Walk half right, away from the railway. The path is faint but clear enough. Pass through a tumbled wall and bear slightly left up the steeper slope, then follow the path, trending slightly rightward, over the crest to a prominent ladder stile. A clearer path beyond this leads across the slope and soon descends to meet the main road opposite a line of cottages. It's probably best to cross right away as the verge on the far side is safer. Turn right, back to the road junction and the parking place.

Hawes and Hardraw

*From busy Hawes to Hardraw, with
a visit to the famous waterfall.*

DISTANCE *5 miles (8km)*   MINIMUM TIME *2hrs*
ASCENT/GRADIENT *426ft (130m)* ▲▲▲   LEVEL OF DIFFICULTY **+++**
PATHS *Field and moorland paths, may be muddy, 35 stiles*
LANDSCAPE *Moorland and farmland*
SUGGESTED MAP *OS Explorer OL30 Yorkshire Dales – Northern & Central*
START/FINISH *Grid reference: SD 870898*
DOG FRIENDLINESS *Dogs under close control throughout; lots of stiles*
PARKING *Pay-and-display car park off Gayle Lane at west side of Hawes*
PUBLIC TOILETS *On main street, just below car park*

For many people, Hawes means two things – Wensleydale cheese and motorcyclists. The bikers use the town as a base at summer weekends and bank holidays, enjoying a friendly drink in the pubs and spectacular rides on the surrounding roads. However, it is the Wensleydale Creamery that attracts other visitors. Just above the car park in Gayle Lane, the Creamery offers tours and tastings, as well as the chance to buy a traditional Wensleydale.

Cheese has been made in Wensleydale since French monks brought the skill here in 1150. After centuries of farm production, a factory was started in Hawes in 1897. It was saved from closure in the 1930s by local man Kit Calvert, and again in 1992, when the local managers bought the creamery from Dairy Crest. It is now a thriving business and a vital part of the Hawes economy.

Force of Nature

The walk gives you the chance – which you should take – to visit the famous Hardraw Force, a 90ft (27m) waterfall in a deep and narrow valley. There is a modest entrance charge, payable in the Green Dragon pub in Hardraw village, and a short, pleasant walk to the falls. Despite appearances, what you see isn't entirely natural. On 12 July 1889 an unprecedented deluge on the hill above caused a wall of water to descend Hardraw Beck and through the valley, destroying buildings in the village and washing away bridges. It also devastated the waterfall, reducing it to a mudslide. After seeing to the clearing up in the village and the welfare of his tenants, the local landowner, Lord Wharncliffe, arranged for his workmen to reconstruct the lip of the fall, pinning together the blocks of shattered stone. This he did so successfully that today's visitors have no idea of the disaster that happened more than a century ago.

Bands in the Valley

On the way to and from Hardraw Force, you will pass the circular bandstand for the annual Hardraw Scar Brass Band Contest, usually held in September.

HAWES

It was founded in 1881, and is reputed to be the second oldest brass band competition in the world. Bands from throughout the North of England – and beyond – compete in the championship, cheered on by supporters who crowd the valley floor and hillsides of this natural amphitheatre.

Old Ropes – and New

From the tiny village of Sedbusk, near the end of the walk, came the area's first-known rope maker, John Brenkley, who died in 1725. The tradition is continued today in Hawes by W R Outhwaite and Son in their Hawes Ropeworks. Visitors can see work in progress on ropes of all types, including ropes for bells, barriers and banisters, as well as dog leads and braids.

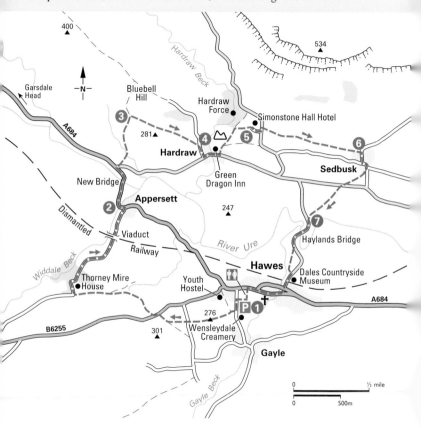

WALK 8 DIRECTIONS

❶ From the car park turn left. Just before the Creamery turn right between houses. Follow the left side of the field to a stile at the top. Keep straight on past a barn and across a lane. After passing a ruined barn, bear right to the B6255. Turn left, then right through a gate signed 'Thorney Mire House'.

Follow the path, which bears left between parallel walls, for 0.5 mile (800m) to meet a lan. Turn right and follow this to the A684 at Appersett.

❷ Turn left over the bridge. Continue over another bridge to a junction, turn right and go straight over a stile, signed 'Bluebell Hill'. Bear slightly right to a gate and over a bridge, then bear left uphill to reach a gate. Continue past waymarks to a signpost.

❸ Turn right and walk to a stile (Bob's Stile) then bear slightly right to a prominent ladder stile. Walk straight ahead and Hardraw soon appears. Continue down over a stile, then over a ladder stile into a lane.

❹ Turn right, then left at the main road. Hardraw Force entrance is through the Green Dragon pub. Immediately after the pub, turn left, then right through a signed gap in the wall and through a courtyard. Follow a flagged path and steps uphill to a house. Turn right behind it, pass right of the stables, then bear slightly left to pass below the grounds of Simonstone Hall Hotel, joining its drive.

❺ Walk down to a road and turn left. Almost immediately turn right through a stile signed 'Sedbusk'. Follow the track past farm buildings to a ladder stile, then continue straight ahead. Skirt below a house and continue over more stiles, along a flagged path and between houses into Sedbusk.

❻ Turn right along the road, bend left near the postbox and descend. Go right, over a stile signed

'Haylands Bridge'. Cross the field, bear right below a wall-corner to a stile, then descend to a stile by the right end of a line of trees. Cross the lane to another stile and follow an obvious path across a stream. Descend to a humpback bridge and continue to a road.

❼ Turn left and cross Haylands Bridge. About 200yds (183m) beyond, go right through a kissing gate signed 'Hawes'. Follow the path to a track, turn left a few paces, then right on to the main road. At the junction, cross the first road, then turn right past the post office. Follow the main road through Hawes. Immediately before the public toilets, turn left up steps to the car park.

Cowgill, a Geologist and the River Dee

An easy walk at the head of Dentdale, in the footsteps of Adam Sedgwick, beside the River Dee and back through farmland.

DISTANCE *3.5 miles (5.7km)*   MINIMUM TIME *1hr 30min*

ASCENT/GRADIENT *131ft (40m)* ▲▲▲   LEVEL OF DIFFICULTY ✦✦✦

PATHS *Tracks, field and riverside paths, some roads, 17 stiles*

LANDSCAPE *Lush valley bottom, views of the fells and farmland*

SUGGESTED MAP *OS Explorer OL2 Yorkshire Dales – Southern & Western*

START/FINISH *Grid reference: SD 742864*

DOG FRIENDLINESS *Keep under close control; lots of stiles*

PARKING *Parking place at Ibbeth Peril*

PUBLIC TOILETS *None en route*

Cowgill, near the narrow head of Dentdale, is a cluster of houses alongside the River Dee. Now mostly an agricultural, holiday and residential settlement, in the past it housed both miners and mill workers – near Ewegales Bridge was Dee Mill, where worsteds were spun at the beginning of the 19th century. The fast-flowing Dee, which may be named after a Celtic river goddess, and in turn gives its name to Dentdale, provided the motive power; it tumbles and slides across limestone terraces and through gorges on its way to join the River Rawthey near Sedbergh. Though innocent in good weather, the river can be fierce after rain – in 1870 Ewegales Bridge and Lea Yeat Bridge, both on the walk, were swept away.

Perilous Undertaking

The start of the walk crosses a footbridge over the river as it rushes through a gorge where there is a waterfall called Ibbeth Peril. The waterfall has a cave (reputedly the home of a witch called Ibby) behind it – just one of a series of caves and passages that riddle the limestone in this part of the dale. Much favoured by speleologists, access to the main system (for the experienced only) is through a narrow entrance in the riverbank, which leads to a passage eventually opening into a large cavern. There are other caverns and underground waterfalls beyond, though the whole system has yet to be explored in full.

The Queen Intervenes

St John's Church at Cowgill, seen across the river near Ewegales Bridge, owes much to geologist Adam Sedgwick (see Walk 6). His sister started a Sunday school in Cowgill at the beginning of the 19th century, and by the 1830s there was a pressing need for a church. Sedgwick himself laid the foundation stone in 1837, when a crowd of 700 gathered in celebration. 'I handled the trowel,' he later wrote, 'and laid the stone, then addressed my countrymen, after which we again uncurled ourselves into a long string to the tune of God Save the King and the strangers, school children, and some others went down to Dent and had cold meat and coffee at the old parsonage. My sister made thirty-six gallons of coffee in a brewing vessel.' The early days of the chapel were not straightforward; diocesan officials first failed to register it as a place of worship at all, then called it by the wrong name. It took the personal intervention of Queen Victoria – Sedgwick had been a close acquaintance of Prince Albert – to sort out the mess.

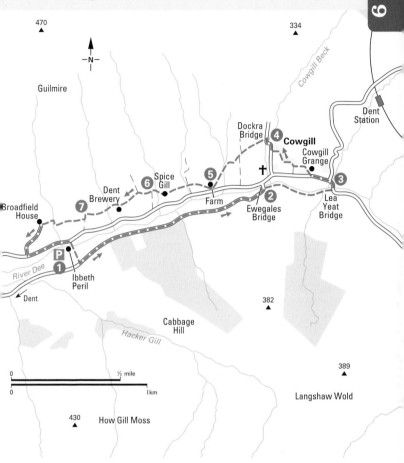

WALK 9 DIRECTIONS

❶ Opposite the car park entrance, a short footpath leads to a footbridge. Cross, then head across the field to a gate and turn left along the road. Follow the road for 1 mile (1.6km) until you get to a stone bridge over the River Dee.

❷ Don't cross the bridge, but go over a stile signed 'Lea Yeat' and continue along the riverside path until a wooden stile leads on to Lea Yeat Bridge. Cross the bridge, then turn left at the signpost towards Dent and Sedbergh.

❸ Just beyond the postbox on the left, follow a sign on the right to Dockra Bridge. Go a short way up the drive for Cowgill Grange, then bear left behind another house to a stile. Continue to walk below another house, then bear

39

right to a gate. Continue through more gates to skirt left of another house and out to a track. Go right and soon reach Dockra Bridge.

④ Cross the bridge, bend right, then go over a stile on your left. Go half left to a stile in a crossing wall. Continue with a wall on your left and cross a track to a waymarked gate. Go right of a barn, through a gateway below a power line and cross a small stream. Bear left across a field to a signpost and stile by a farm.

WHERE TO EAT AND DRINK
There is nowhere immediately on the route, so head for Dent, with its two pubs and four tea rooms, or go east towards Dent Head viaduct for the Sportsman's Inn, which serves bar meals. It is usually closed in the afternoons.

⑤ Go half right to another stile. Continue along a wall to another stile and footbridge, then head towards farm buildings. Follow the track through the farmyard, then turn right immediately after the farmhouse, before a stone barn. Go left behind the barn to a bridge with steps and a gated stile beyond.

⑥ Cross the field to another stile in the corner. Just beyond, turn

right along a track. As it bends right, go straight ahead to pass below a house and down to a gate. Go round behind another house to a wooden stile. Go ahead across the field to a stone stile, then go left of the barn on to a track over a stream.

⑦ Curve round left of the next barn and follow the wall. At the next farm buildings, go through a metal gate by a barn, then follow the walled, often wet, track bending right. At the next gate bear left, go through a stile, go to the right of the farm building and on to a track. Turn right, bear left through a waymarked gate, pass the farmhouse and follow the track to the road. Turn left to return to the car park; you can join a parallel path through the trees near the end.

WHILE YOU'RE THERE
Visit Dent Brewery, which you pass on the walk at Hollins. It is not open to casual visitors – so don't just drop in – but visits are available every Saturday, starting from the George and Dragon in Dent, with transport to the brewery. You can sample some of the Brewery's prize-winning beers, many with sheep-related names such as Sheep and Shearful, Baarister and Ewe are the Weakest Link.

WHAT TO LOOK OUT FOR
While on the first, eastward, part of the walk, look up to the facing hillside to see the white-painted Victorian buildings of Dent Station – the highest mainline railway station in England. It is 1,132ft (345m) above sea level and is one of the stops on the spectacular Settle-to-Carlisle line. While it can be an inhospitable place when the winds blow and the winter storms set in, it proved a way into the wider world for the people of Dentdale – even though to reach it from Dent meant a 4-mile (6.4km) walk and a stiff climb. In the later part of his life it was the route regularly taken by Adam Sedgwick (see Walk 6) on his way to and from York to reach London or Cambridge. It is still used by local people today – you may see them walking along the valley roads carrying their supermarket shopping from Settle or Carlisle. And you will certainly hear the whistle of the trains as they pass over Dent Head and Arten Gill viaducts as they approach Dent Station.

Semer Water – A Legendary Glacial Lake

*Legends — perhaps with a basis in dim and distant truth —
surround Yorkshire's biggest natural lake.*

DISTANCE 5 miles (8km)	MINIMUM TIME 2hrs 15min

DISTANCE 5 miles (8km)   MINIMUM TIME 2hrs 15min

ASCENT/GRADIENT 853ft (260m) ▲▲▲   LEVEL OF DIFFICULTY +++

PATHS Field paths and tracks, steep ascent from Marsett, 16 stiles

LANDSCAPE Valley, lake and fine views over Wensleydale

SUGGESTED MAP OS Explorer OL30 Yorkshire Dales – Northern & Central

START/FINISH Grid reference: SD 921875

DOG FRIENDLINESS Dogs should be on leads

PARKING Car park at the north end of the lake: fee payable at Low Blean
farm nearby

PUBLIC TOILETS None en route

Semer Water was formed as the result of the end of the last ice age. Glacial meltwater attempted to drain away down the valley the glacier had gouged out of the limestone, but was prevented from doing so by a wall of boulder clay, dumped by the glacier itself, across the valley's end. So the water built up, forming a lake which once stretched 3 miles (4.8km) up Raydale. Natural silting has gradually filled the upper part of the lake bed, leaving Semer Water – at 0.5 mile (800m) long – North Yorkshire's largest natural lake.

Legendary Semer Water

Semer Water boasts several legends. One concerns the three huge blocks of limestone deposited by the departing glacier at the water's edge at the north end. Called the Carlow Stone and the Mermaid Stones, they are said to have landed here when the Devil and a giant who lived on Addlebrough, the prominent hill a mile (1.6km) to the east, began lobbing missiles at each other. More famous is the story of the beggar who came to the town that once stood where the lake is now. He went from door to door, asking for food and drink, but was refused by everyone – except the poorest couple. Revealing himself as an angel, he raised his staff over the town, crying 'Semer Water rise, Semer Water sink, and swallow all save this little house, that gave me meat and drink.' The waters overwhelmed the town, leaving the poor people's cottage on the brink of the new lake. Some say the church bells can still be heard ringing beneath the waters.

Behind the Legend

There are indeed the remains of a settlement beneath Semer Water. Houses perched on stilts were built along the water's edge in iron age times, though there may have been an earlier settlement here in neolithic times, too, for flint arrow heads have been found. A Bronze Age spear head was found in 1937 when the lake's waters were lowered.

Setts and Quakers

Marsett, at the lake's southern end, and Countersett, to the north, both end with the Old Norse word denoting a place of hill pasture. Marsett is a hamlet of old farmhouses, and on the road to Countersett, at Carr End, is the house where Dr Fothergill was born in 1712.

A famous Quaker philanthropist, he founded the Quaker school at Ackworth in South Yorkshire. The American statesman Benjamin Franklin said he found it hard to believe that any better man than Fothergill had ever lived. Countersett has one of several old Friends' Meeting Houses in Wensleydale, and the Hall was home, in the 17th century, to Richard Robinson, who was responsible for the spread of Quakerism in the Dales.

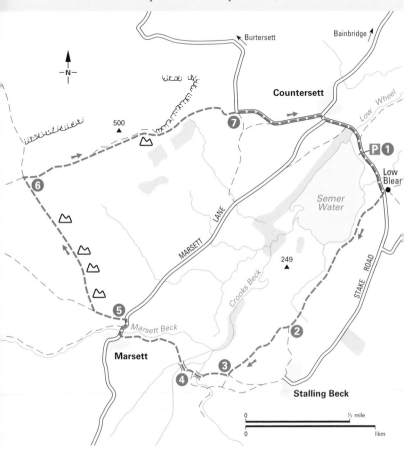

WALK 10 DIRECTIONS

❶ Turn right from the car park up the road. Opposite Low Blean farm, go right over a stile, signed 'Stalling Busk'. Cross another stile and continue towards a barn. Pass right of it to find a clearer path. Follow this, leaving the lake behind and passing a Wildlife Trust sign. Continue past an information board and then skirt above an old graveyard to a gate and signpost just beyond.

❷ Follow the Marsett sign into the field corner and cross a gated stile. Follow the level path through

SEMER WATER

more stiles, then across a larger field, keeping just above a steeper slope. Pass right of a barn among trees, then cross a stream bed.

❸ Bear right immediately on a narrow path, descending gently above a roofless barn to a stile. Continue to a stile at the corner of another barn, then turn right immediately across a level meadow, with a wall on your right. Cross the wall at a gate, then follow it to a footbridge. Cross and go straight ahead to another footbridge beside a ford.

WHAT TO LOOK OUT FOR

Semer Water offers a wide variety of habitats for wildlife. The waters of the lake, which have a high plankton content, support many fish including bream and perch, as well as crayfish. Water birds include great crested grebe and tufted duck. You may also occasionally see Whooper swans. Over the fringes of the lake, dragonflies and damsel flies can be seen glittering in the summer. On the wet margins of the lake grow flowers such as marsh marigold, marsh cinquefoil, ragged robin and valerian, while in the dryer areas the wood anemone is frequently found. Birds such as lapwings, redshank and reed bunting may also be seen, while summer visitors include the sandmartin.

❹ Continue along the obvious track, meeting another river. Approaching Marsett, bear right across a green, following the stream, to a red telephone box. Turn right over the bridge. 100yds (91m) beyond, take a track signed 'Burtersett and Hawes' (not the path by the river).

❺ Walk uphill to a gate on the right where the wire fence ends. Cross the stile and climb a faint

WALK 10

WHILE YOU'RE THERE

Visit Bainbridge, with its wide green and attractive houses. The Romans had a fort here, Virosidum, on top of the hill called Brough. The River Bain, crossed by the bridge which gives the village its name, is England's shortest river, running all of 2 miles (3.2km) from Semer Water to the River Ure.

but direct (and generally steep) path. Reaching a ladder stile with an Access Land symbol, go straight ahead up a final steep slope, then more easily on a green path to a crossing track just below the final crest.

❻ Turn right along the track to a gate on the skyline. Continue along the track to a green knoll with views to the west. Descend to a gate, then follow the track more steeply downhill, winding below crags then slanting down the slope on a grooved track. Follow the track as it bends right and back left to reach a road.

WHERE TO EAT AND DRINK

The nearest place to Semer Water is Bainbridge, where the Rose and Crown Hotel by the Green dates back more than 500 years. The Bainbridge Horn, blown to guide travellers to the village in the dark winter months, hangs here. The hotel serves home-cooked local produce both in the bars and, in the evening, in the Dales Room Restaurant.

❼ Turn right and follow the road downhill to a staggered crossroads on the edge of Countersett. Turn right, then left, signed 'Stalling Busk'. Descend the lane over the bridge and back to the car park.

Villages, Falls and Intriguing Follies

From West Burton to Aysgarth and back, via the famous Aysgarth Falls and some unusual farm buildings.

DISTANCE 4 miles (6.4km)	MINIMUM TIME 1hr 30min
ASCENT/GRADIENT 394ft (120m) ▲▲▲	LEVEL OF DIFFICULTY +++

PATHS Field and riverside paths and tracks, 35 stiles

LANDSCAPE Two typical dales villages, fields and falls on the River Ure

SUGGESTED MAP OS Explorer OL30 Yorkshire Dales – Northern & Central

START/FINISH Grid reference: SE 017867

DOG FRIENDLINESS Dogs should be on leads

PARKING Centre of West Burton, by (but not on) the Green

PUBLIC TOILETS None en route; Aysgarth National Park visitor centre is close

Many people regard West Burton as the prettiest village in the Dales. Its wide, irregular green, with a fat obelisk of 1820, is surrounded by small stone cottages, formerly homes to quarrymen and miners – but no church. Villagers had to make the trek to Aysgarth for services. West Burton has always been an important centre. It is at the entrance to Bishopdale, with its road link to Wharfedale. South is the road to Walden Head, now a dead end for motorists, but for walkers an alternative route to Starbotton and Kettlewell. At the end of the walk you'll travel for a short time, near Flanders Hall, along Morpeth Gate, the old packhorse route to Middleham.

Two Halves of Aysgarth

After crossing the wide flood plain of Bishopdale Beck, and crossing Eshington Bridge, you climb across the hill to descend into Aysgarth. A village of two halves, the larger part, which you come to first, is set along the main A684 road. The walk takes you along the traditional field path from this part of the village to its other half, set around St Andrew's Church. It's worth looking inside; it contains the spectacular choir screen brought here from Jervaulx Abbey, down the dale, when it was closed by Henry VIII. Like the elaborate stall beside it, it was carved by the renowned Ripon workshops.

The Falls and the Wood

Beyond the church, the path follows the river beside Aysgarth's Middle and Lower Falls. The Falls were formed by the Ure eating away at the underlying limestone as it descends from Upper Wensleydale to join the deeper Bishopdale. They are now one of the most popular tourist sights in the Yorkshire Dales National Park and the Upper Falls, by the bridge, featured in the film *Robin Hood, Prince of Thieves*.

Mrs Sykes' Follies

On the return leg of the walk, you pass below two oddities in the parkland behind the house at Sorrellsykes Park. These two follies were built in the 18th century by Mrs Sykes and no one seems to knows why.

WEST BURTON

One is a round tower, with a narrowing waist like a diabolo. The other, sitting like Thunderbird 3 ready for lift-off, is known to local people as the 'Rocket Ship'. It is of no practical use, except for minimal shelter in the square room in its base, but it is just one of many folly cones throughout Britain. None of the others, however, have this elaborate arrangement of fins – presumably added because the builder had doubts about its stability.

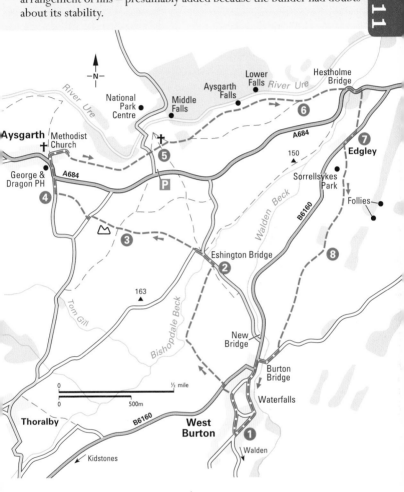

WALK 11 DIRECTIONS

❶ Leave the Green near the village shop. Opposite 'Meadowcroft' go left, signed 'Eshington Bridge'. Cross the road, turn right, then left through a gate and down steps. Go through a gate beside a barn and continue to a stile at the bottom right of the field. Cross two more stiles, then bear right to meet a stone wall.

Follow this then continue in the same direction to a road.

❷ Turn left, cross the bridge and go up a narrow lane to a bend. Go ahead through a stile, signed 'Aysgarth'. Climb past another stile and left of a barn. Continue up the field and bear left to a gate near the corner, then diagonally across the next field. Keep left of an obvious wall-gap to a stile by another gap. Descend to a stile and footpath sign.

3 Continue in the same direction and up to a signpost. Follow the Aysgarth direction to a gateway and stile. Cross the field half left to a stile onto a lane. Turn left, then right, signed 'Aysgarth'. Go through three stiles to a road.

4 Turn right, into the village. Go past the George and Dragon then straight ahead to the Methodist Church and bear right along the lane. Cross a stile by Field House. Follow the wall and continue along a short track, then follow a path through eight stiles to a road.

5 Enter the churchyard, pass right of the church and leave by a stile. Cross a field and go through a wood. Follow the path downhill, descending steps to the river bank. Take a signed stile right.

6 Follow the path by the river to a signpost. Bend right across a field to the main road. Turn left, cross a bridge, then turn right into woodland, signed 'Edgley', soon bearing left, uphill, to a stile. Bear right across a field to a gate in the far corner and join a road.

7 Turn right. About 150yds (137m) along, go left over a stile, signed 'Flanders Hall'. Walk towards the follies, then bear right just below the ridge, passing

Sorrelsykes Park to your right. Cross a track and bear left past a waymark to a signpost. Turn right to a stepped stone stile, then follow the bottom edge of the field to reach a gate opposite a stone barn.

8 Descend through this and two more gates, then bear left along the field edge to a stile. Continue ahead to a lane. Turn right, cross a bridge and join the village road. Turn left, back to the Green.

A Kingdom for a Horse

*From Middleham Castle, favourite home of King Richard III,
and back via the gallops for today's thoroughbreds.*

DISTANCE	7 miles (11.3km) MINIMUM TIME 2hrs 30min
ASCENT/GRADIENT	475ft (145m) ▲▲▲ LEVEL OF DIFFICULTY +++
PATHS	Field paths and tracks, with some road walking, 14 stiles
LANDSCAPE	Gentle farmland, riverside paths, views of Wensleydale
SUGGESTED MAP	OS Explorer OL30 Yorkshire Dales – Northern & Central
START/FINISH	Grid reference: SE 127877
DOG FRIENDLINESS	Livestock and horses in fields, so dogs on leads
PARKING	In square in centre of Middleham
PUBLIC TOILETS	Middleham

When Richard III died at the battle of Bosworth Field in 1485, Middleham lost one of its favourite residents. Richard had lived here – in the household of the Earl of Warwick – The Kingmaker – when a boy, and set up home here with the Earl's daughter Anne after their marriage. As Duke of Gloucester, it was his power base as effective ruler of the North under his brother Edward IV. Locals don't believe the propagandist version of Richard, promoted by Shakespeare's play, that he was a murderer – the Lord Mayor of York reported to his council after Bosworth that 'King Richard, late lawfully reigning over us, was through great treason piteously slain and murdered.' Middleham Castle today is a splendid ruin, with one of the biggest keeps in England, impressive curtain walls and a deep moat. It is in the care of English Heritage.

From Middleham, the walk takes us to the River Cover and along its banks. After crossing Hullo Bridge, the path passes near Braithwaite Hall. Owned by the National Trust and open by appointment only, this is a modest farmhouse of 1667, with three fine gables and unusual oval windows beneath them. Inside are stone-flagged floors, a fine oak staircase and wood panelling, all of the late 17th century. On the hillside behind are the earthworks of a hill fort, thought to be iron age. After the Hall, the lane eventually crosses Coverham Bridge, probably built by the monks of nearby Coverham Abbey. There are a few remains of the Abbey, founded in the 12th century, mostly incorporated into later buildings on the site. Miles Coverdale, who was the first man to complete a full English translation of the Bible, came from here.

Middleham – the Lambourne of the North

For many people, Middleham is the home of famous racehorses, and you may be lucky enough to see some in training as you walk over Middleham Low Moor towards the end of the walk – make sure you keep out of their way. More than 500 horses train in Middleham, under the watchful eyes of 13 trainers. Both the Low Moor and the High Moor have been used for exercise for more than 300 years; one of the earliest recorded winners was Bay Bolton, born in 1705, which won Queen Anne's Gold Cup at York Races. Among early jockeys was the splendidly-named 'Crying Jackie' Mangle, who won the St Leger five times in the 1770s and 80s.

To your left as you leave the Low Moor and make your way back to the castle is William's Hill, the remains of the original motte and bailey castle built here by the Normans after 1066 to guard the approaches to Wensleydale and Coverdale. The motte, 40ft (12m) high, is joined by a curved bailey surrounded by a ditch. It was abandoned in 1170 when the new castle was begun near by.

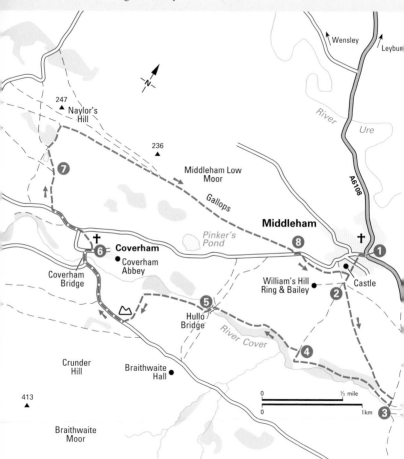

WALK 12 DIRECTIONS

❶ From the square, take the Coverham road then turn left up a passage beside the Castle Keep Tea Rooms. Continue left of the Castle along a walled track to a gate.

❷ Bear left across the big field, following the sign for 'stepping

stones'. Cross two more fields, over waymarked stiles. After the third stile, follow the field edge above a steep bank. At a crossing wall turn right, down to the River Cover by the stepping stones.

❸ Turn right (do not cross the river) and follow the path through woods and a field. A gate leads to steps and an elevated section. After returning to the riverbank, cross a stile into a field. After another stile at its end, turn immediately right. Climb steeply to a marker post.

4 Turn left and follow the edge of a wood. At the end of the field, go left through the trees, then straight ahead on an obvious descending path. Cross a stile and turn left to Hullo Bridge.

WHAT TO LOOK OUT FOR

If you are very lucky you may see the iridescent blue and orange of the kingfisher, fishing above the waters of the River Cover. Vulnerable both to pollution and the ravages of a harsh winter, the kingfisher lives in the banks of the river, digging out a burrow up to 3ft (1m) deep. At the end, a nest is constructed for the female to lay six or seven eggs. Young kingfishers are fed mainly with small fish – minnow and sticklebacks. Kingfishers catch fish with their fearsome bills and carry them back to their perches overlooking the stream. They carefully turn them so the head faces outwards from the bill, and hit them against the perch to stun or kill them, before swallowing them whole.

5 Cross the bridge and turn right on a permissive path, crossing three stiles. At a crossing wire fence turn left. Cross another stile. Where the fence bends right, go ahead up a steep bank to reach a gate on to a lane. Turn right and descend to Coverham Bridge. Cross the bridge and turn right on a track.

6 Before iron gates, turn left through a small gate, climbing beside a waterfall into the churchyard. Leave by the lychgate and bear left along the main road (signed to Forbidden Corner). After 0.25 mile (400m), go through a

WHERE TO EAT AND DRINK

Several of Middleham's hotels and inns offer meals and snacks as well as drinks. The White Swan has bar meals and a noted Brasserie, open lunchtime and evenings. The Richard III has a varied bar menu, specialising in sausages. The Castle Keep and The Nosebag are both good, friendly tearooms.

gate on the right opposite a disused factory. Bear slightly left, cross three stiles, then aim for a prominent gap between buildings and continue through a narrow strip of woodland.

7 Bear slightly left to a stile, right of a stone wall. Skirt ornamental ponds to meet a track. Turn right and ascend past a house to a gateway onto a wider track. Turn right. Where the track bends right, keep straight ahead across the grassy moor; look for occasional blue-topped posts marking the line of a bridleway. When the long fenced gallops appear, keep them to your left and continue down to the road.

8 Turn left. Just before the Middleham sign, take a signposted path on the right. Cross the stile, turn left and follow the path parallel to the road. Go through a stile and a gate, then bear left down to another stile and through a gate on to the lane. Turn left and return to the square.

WHILE YOU'RE THERE

Nearby Wensley, after which the dale takes its name, was once a market town, but plague in 1563 reduced it to this little village. Visit the church to see the monumental brass to the priest Simon de Wensley – one of the best in the country – and the wonderful out-of-place Scrope family pew, partly made of the rood screen from Easby Abbey near Richmond.

Whittington Without a Cat

A walk from Kirkby Lonsdale, returning along the banks of the River Lune.

DISTANCE 4.75 miles (7.7km)	**MINIMUM TIME** 2hrs 30min

ASCENT/GRADIENT 197ft (60m) ▲▲▲ **LEVEL OF DIFFICULTY** +++

PATHS *A little overgrown and indistinct in patches, quiet lanes and tracks, 12 stiles*

LANDSCAPE *Rolling hills, farmland, riverbank, good distance views*

SUGGESTED MAP *OS Explorer OL2 Yorkshire Dales – Southern & Western*

START/FINISH *Grid reference: SD 615782*

DOG FRIENDLINESS *On lead through farmland*

PARKING *Devil's Bridge car park, Kirkby Lonsdale (free of charge)*

PUBLIC TOILETS *At the start*

It's something of a revelation, to escape the weekend motorcycle congregation on Devil's Bridge and take this circular walk over rolling hills, through farmland and woods, to the worthy village of Whittington, then to return along the banks of the lovely Lune. You pass close to Sellet Mill – its huge waterwheel, incorporated within the building, was reputedly once the second largest in the country. Corn was ground at the mill until its closure in the 1940s. Sellet is a word you'll come across often on this walk and is apparently an old local word for drumlin (a small rounded hill formed by glacial deposits). Your next Sellet is Sellet Bank, which appears to be a large drumlin. The walk takes you around its base and eventually to Sellet Hall. Built as a farm in 1570 by the Baines family, the hall was possibly used at sometime as a hospital, as it is situated at the end of Hosticle Lane – hosticle is an old dialect word for hospital. You return to Kirkby Lonsdale along the banks of the River Lune, following part of the Lune Valley Ramble.

The Devil's Bridge

A simple spring in a field at Newbiggin-on-Lune is the source of the beautiful River Lune, which eventually flows into Morecambe Bay and the Irish Sea to the north of Cockersand Abbey. The river has inspired many artists, most famously J M W Turner, who visited Kirkby Lonsdale in 1818 and subsequently included the river in two of his paintings. The riverbed is rocky under Devil's Bridge, so called because it was supposedly provided by the Devil to enable a poor widow to reach her cow on the other side of the river. In return for this, the Devil was to acquire the soul of the first being to cross the bridge. The widow's only other possession was a small dog. According to a popular poem from the 1820s, she threw a bun across the bridge and the poor hound scampered after it, thus thwarting the Devil and saving her own soul. This graceful, three arched monument probably dates from the 14th century and no longer has to support the busy A65, which has had its own river crossing a short way downstream since the 1930s.

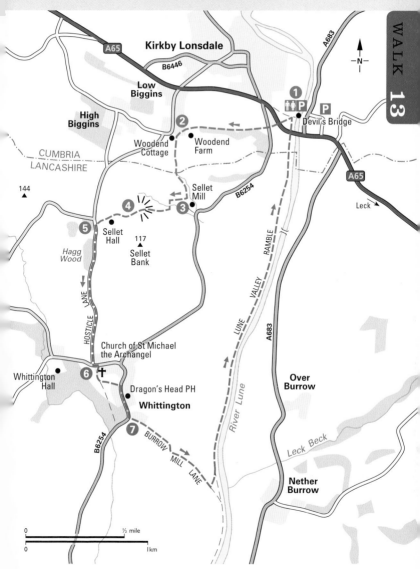

WALK 13 DIRECTIONS

❶ From the west bank of the river, a few paces downstream from Devil's Bridge, go diagonally up across a park with picnic tables to a kissing gate near paired conifers. Cross the A65, go through a narrow meadow and between houses and cross the B6254. As you enter another meadow, go uphill, keeping the walled wooded area on your left. Yellow markers help you find the route. Keep on over the brow of the hill and straight ahead through two kissing gates to a metal gate near houses. Bear left to a signpost.

❷ Cross a farm track and walk in front of white-painted Woodend Cottage to enter a walled path. This is remarkably rough in places. Lower down, a stream comes in from the left and tries

51

to take over the path, but you can escape rightwards to drier ground before the millpond of Sellet Mill. Continue past sheds to a farmyard.

❸ Turn right over a stile and walk up the field, keeping the fence to your left, until just past the end of a garden. Go left through a yellow marked gate and walk straight across a small field to another marked gate followed immediately by a shallow stream. Turn right to go round Sellet Bank, aiming initially for the corner of a hedge under power-lines. Continue with the hedge to your right, taking time to look back at good views of Leck Fell and Barbon Fell.

WHAT TO LOOK OUT FOR

Leck Fell at 2,058ft (627m) is the highest point in present day Lancashire (although Coniston Old Man is the highest point in the 'old' Lancashire). The fell is worth visiting for its limestone scenery and archaeological sites, while below ground is a popular network of caving systems.

---

❹ As the hedge begins to bear left, cross it through a yellow marked stile on your right, then skirt round a wooded area. Facing Sellet Hall, turn right adjacent to the fenced driveway following the marker arrows, then keep on over the corner of the field to cross a stile and drop down a couple of steps to the road at a T-junction. Turn left along Hosticle Lane towards Whittington village.

❺ The lane is sunken in places and carries very little traffic. The descent steepens as you approach the outskirts of Whittington.

❻ Go left at the T-junction for a few paces, then cross the road and turn right over a pebbled mosaic at the entrance to the Church of

---

WHILE YOU'RE THERE

Visit Kirkby Lonsdale which has a market charter from the 13th century and still holds a weekly market, around the unusual 20th-century butter cross, every Thursday. There are some fine 17th- and 18th-century buildings and the famous views from the churchyard.

St Michael the Archangel. Keep the square bell tower on your left before descending stone steps to go through a narrow stile and the modern graveyard. Follow the hedge to a gate in the left corner and keep straight on to reach a stone stile into a walled path that leads on to Main Street. Turn right and walk through the village past the village hall and the Dragon's Head pub.

❼ At a sharp right bend on the edge of the village, turn left along a gritty track, passing a farm and tennis courts. Follow the lane as it winds between fields, eventually crossing a cattle grid and running out at an anglers' hut beside the Lune. Follow the riverbank upstream on the route of the Lune Valley Ramble. There's a short overgrown section but it soon becomes an easy walk through fields, always close to the river. The route is obvious back to the A65 bridge at Kirkby Lonsdale. Go through a gate and up steps to the left of the parapet. Cross the road and drop down the other side to cross the park at the start of the walk.

WHERE TO EAT AND DRINK

There are usually a couple of vans at Devil's Bridge, one selling ices and the other drinks and snacks. The Dragon's Head pub in Whittington opens from 12 noon to 3pm every lunchtime except Monday and serves a selection of hot and cold food.

Around Ribblehead's Majestic Viaduct

Beside and beneath a great
monument to Victorian engineering.

DISTANCE *5 miles (8km)*   MINIMUM TIME *2hrs*

ASCENT/GRADIENT *328ft (100m)* ▲▲▲   LEVEL OF DIFFICULTY +++

PATHS *Moorland and farm paths and tracks, 1 stile*

LANDSCAPE *Bleak moorland and farmland, dominated by the Ribblehead viaduct*

SUGGESTED MAP *OS Explorer OL2 Yorkshire Dales – Southern & Western*

START/FINISH *Grid reference: SD 765792*

DOG FRIENDLINESS *Dogs can be off lead by viaduct, but should be on leads in farmland*

PARKING *Parking space at junction of B6255 and B6479 near Ribblehead viaduct*

PUBLIC TOILETS *None en route*

‘Nowhere in the kingdom has nature placed such gigantic obstacles in the way of the railway engineer’, observed a newspaper when the Settle-to-Carlisle railway line was complete. The railway was planned and built by the Midland Railway so it could reach Scotland without trespassing on its rivals’ territory of the east or west coast routes. It cost the then enormous sum of £3,500,000 and was opened in 1876. Its construction included building 20 big viaducts and 14 tunnels. At the height of the works, 6,000 men were employed, living in shanty towns beside the line and giving the area a flavour of the Wild West. The line survived for almost 100 years, until passenger services were withdrawn in 1970 amongst claims Ribblehead was unsafe. There was a public outcry which led to a concerted campaign to keep the line open. Ribblehead is now repaired, and the line is one of the most popular – and spectacular – tourist lines in the country.

Ribblehead – 'A Mighty Work'

It took five years to build Ribblehead's huge viaduct. It is 0.25 mile (400m) long, and is 100ft (30m) high at its maximum; the columns stretch another 25ft (7.6m) into the ground. The stone – more than 30,000 cubic yards (22,950 cubic m) of it – came from Littledale, and construction progressed from north to south. The area is called Batty Moss, and was inhospitable, to say the least. There is a rumour that the columns are set on bales of wool, as the engineers could not find the bedrock. This, romantic as it is in a county whose fortunes are largely based on wool, is untrue; they are set in concrete on top of the rock below. There are 24 spans, each 45ft (13.7m) wide. Every sixth column is thicker than its neighbours so that if one column fell it would take only five others with it, and not the whole viaduct.

Blea Moor and Ancient Farms

The walk takes you past the viaduct to the beginning of Blea Moor, and near perhaps the most exposed signal box in Britain. Beyond it is Blea Moor tunnel, another of the mighty engineering works of the Settle-to-

53

RIBBLEHEAD

Carlisle Railway, 2,629yds (2,404m) long and dug by miners working by candlelight. The advent of the miners and the huge paraphernalia of Victorian engineering must have seemed astonishing to the farmers sheltering at the foot of Whernside.

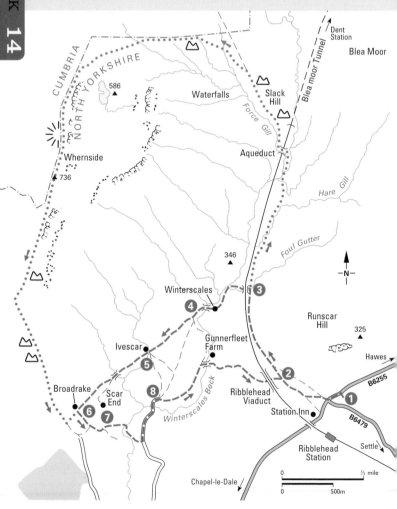

WALK 14 DIRECTIONS

❶ From your parking place near the road junction, with the B6479 at your back, follow green paths towards the viaduct. Turn right on a gravel track and follow it until it turns under the viaduct; continue walking straight ahead.

❷ Walk parallel with the railway line above you to your left, past

a Three Peaks signboard. Go through a gate and continue until you reach a railway signal. Go left under the railway arch, following the public bridleway sign.

❸ Follow the track downhill towards the stream, then bear left, roughly parallel to the water, to Winterscales. Go through a gate between the buildings and on to a humpback bridge below a cottage.

4 Follow the lane over a cattle grid then fork right (almost straight ahead). Keep left at the next fork, pass an isolated cowshed and continue to Ivescar farm. Pass in front of the house and after a few paces bear left through a waymarked gate.

WHILE YOU'RE THERE
Take the road – or the train – up to Dent Station. You will pass through the Blea Moor tunnel and then over the Dent Head viaduct, with its 10 spans, and the same maximum height as Ribblehead. The village of Dent is more than 4 miles (6.4km) from the station!

WHERE TO EAT AND DRINK
In the summer months an ice cream van stations itself at the parking space by the road junction, and it's usually there on weekends in winter too for hot drinks and snacks. The Station Inn, near the viaduct, offers warmth and home-cooked meals in its bar and dining room.

8 Where the road divides, go right, through a gate, towards the viaduct. At the next gate, go right again over a footbridge by the farm buildings. Continue along the track and go under the viaduct, then retrace your steps to the parking place.

EXTENDING THE WALK
You can extend this walk to take in one of the famous Three Peaks, Whernside. From Point **3**, follow the signpost to Dent. Cross over two streams and then the railway by a bridge alongside an aqueduct. Go through a gate, and at a signpost continue ahead for Dentdale (not Dent Head). The path ascends past a waterfall, then climbs steeply to a stile on your left. Turn left over the stile, following the Whernside sign. The path meets a wall on the right and a paved section climbs to the ridge. Continue along the ridge to the summit, then follow the same path steeply downhill to reach two gated stiles, then a pair of ladder stiles flanking a farm gate. Continue down to a farm gate beside a barn, then turn left, signed 'Winterscales'. Follow the path through the field towards the farm. Go through a gate to rejoin the main walk at Point **6**.

5 Walk along a track through fields and cross a small bridge of railway sleepers. Immediately after this, bear right to a small gate. Cross a series of fields, keeping a straight course, to reach Broadrake farm.

6 Turn left down the farm track. Where it bends right, go over the cattle grid and turn sharp left round the fence and on to a track, following the bridleway sign, to a ladder stile.

7 The obvious track winds through fields to reach a stream-bed (usually dry in summer). Cross this, which can be tricky after prolonged wet weather. The track is a little indistinct after the crossing, but bear right, staying near the stream until it becomes clear again. Meet a road near a cattle grid, turn left and walk down the road and over a bridge.

WHAT TO LOOK OUT FOR
On a fine summer's day Ribblehead can seem a magical place but it can be one of the bleakest places in the Dales. The average rainfall in the area is 70 inches (177.8cm) and snow frequently blocks the roads. Wind speeds of 50 knots are a normal occurrence, and gales can reach a greater speed.

Overleaf: The 24-arch Ribblehead viaduct crosses the valley of the River Ribble (Walk 14)

Dalesfolk Traditions in Hubberholme

From JB Priestley's favourite Dales village, along Langstrothdale and back via a limestone terrace.

DISTANCE 5.25 miles (8.4km)   MINIMUM TIME 2hrs

ASCENT/GRADIENT 480ft (146m) ▲▲▲   LEVEL OF DIFFICULTY +++

PATHS Field paths and tracks, steep after Yockenthwaite, 11 stiles

LANDSCAPE Streamside paths and limestone terrace

SUGGESTED MAP OS Explorer OL30 Yorkshire Dales – Northern & Central

START/FINISH Grid reference: SD 927782

DOG FRIENDLINESS Dogs should be on lead, except on section between Yockenthwaite and Cray

PARKING Beside river in village, opposite church (not church parking)

PUBLIC TOILETS None en route

Literary pilgrims visit Hubberholme to see the George Inn, where JB Priestley could often be found enjoying the local ale, and the churchyard, the last resting place for his ashes, as he requested. He chose an idyllic spot. Set at the foot of Langstrothdale, Hubberholme is a cluster of old farmhouses and cottages surrounding the church. Norman in origin, St Michael's was once flooded so badly that fish were seen swimming in the nave. One vicar of Hubberholme is said to have carelessly baptised a child Amorous instead of Ambrose, a mistake that, once entered in the parish register, couldn't be altered. Amorous Stanley used his memorable name later in life as part of his stock-in-trade as a hawker.

Church Wood

Hubberholme church's best treasures are of wood. The rood loft above the screen is one of only two surviving in Yorkshire, (the other is at Flamborough, far away on the east coast). Once holding figures of Christ on the Cross, St Mary and St John, it dates from 1558, when such examples of Popery were fast going out of fashion. It still retains some of its once-garish colouring of red, gold and black. Master-carver Robert Thompson provided almost all the rest of the furniture in 1934 – look for his mouse trademark on each piece.

Ancient Yockenthwaite and Remote Cray

Yockenthwaite's name, said to have been derived from an ancient Irish name, Eogan, conjures up images of the ancient past. Norse settlers were here more than 1,000 years ago and even earlier settlers have left their mark – a Bronze Age stone circle a little further up the valley. The hamlet now consists of a few farm buildings beside the bridge over the Wharfe at the end of Langstrothdale Chase, a Norman hunting ground which used to have its own forest laws and punishments. You walk along a typical Dales limestone terrace to reach Cray, on the road over from Bishopdale joining Wharfedale to Wensleydale. Here is another huddle of farmhouses, around

HUBBERHOLME

the White Lion Inn. You then follow the Cray Gill downstream, past a series of small cascades. For a more spectacular waterfall, head a little way up the road from the inn to Cray High Bridge.

Burning the Candle

Back in Hubberholme, the George Inn was once the vicarage. It is the scene each New Year's Day of an ancient auction. It begins with the lighting of a candle, after which the auctioneer asks for bids for the year's tenancy of the 'Poor Pasture', a 16 acre (6.5ha) field behind the inn. All bids have to be completed before the candle burns out. In the days when the George housed the vicar, he ran the auction. Today a local auctioneer takes the role, and a merry time is had by all. The proceeds from the auction go to help the old people of the village.

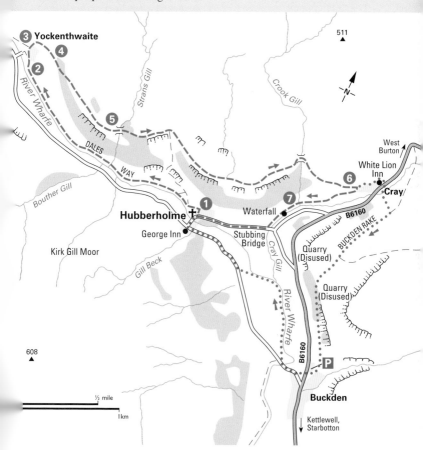

WALK 15 DIRECTIONS

❶ Enter the farmyard beside the church and turn left immediately through a Dales Way signed gate. Take the lower path, signed 'Yockenthwaite', alongside the churchyard. Walk beside the river for 1.25 miles (2km); the clear Dales Way path is never far from the river. Approaching Yockenthwaite, go up steps to a little gate and left to a gate and signpost.

WALK 15

2 Follow the track towards a bridge but, before reaching it, go sharp right up a farm track, which swings back left to a sign to Cray and Hubberholme.

3 Go up to another signpost, then follow the obvious track slanting right and up. Part-way up the hill, go right at a footpath sign through a gate.

4 Follow the near-level path to a signpost, then bear left and up a rough section to another signpost. Turn right and follow the obvious path, descending along a beautiful natural terrace until the path goes left and up to enter a wood by a footbridge over a miniature gorge.

5 Walk through the wood then continue, level again, to reach a small side valley above a house. A signpost above the house points towards Cray. Go up slightly, over rocks, then along another green terrace path for about a mile (1.6km) to a footbridge. Cross this, then ascend slightly to a barn; bear right to a gate then follow a marked path across meadow land. Go past a house to a junction of tracks on the edge of Cray.

6 Go sharp right, down to a footpath sign to Stubbing Bridge. Descend between stone walls and through a gate and on to the grassy hillside. Pass another footpath sign and continue downhill to meet the stream.

7 Follow the streamside path past waterfalls and pools, crossing a stone bridge over a side-stream. Cross a stile and continue past a barn to reach the road. Turn right back to the parking place in Hubberholme.

EXTENDING THE WALK

You can see more of the beautiful Upper Wharfedale scenery by extending Walk 38 from Cray to the peaceful village of Buckden. From Point **6** on the main walk, follow a metalled road to the White Lion Inn, then cross the valley and climb to Buckden Rake. Descend this to Buckden before returning to the car parking place at Hubberholme via the Dales Way.

Horsehouse and Coverdale

*A moorside and riverside walk in one
of the loveliest valleys in the Dales.*

DISTANCE	6.5 miles (10.4km)
MINIMUM TIME	2hrs 30min
ASCENT/GRADIENT	459ft (140m) ▲▲▲
LEVEL OF DIFFICULTY	+++
PATHS	Field, moorland and riverside paths and tracks, 31 stiles
LANDSCAPE	Farmed valley and moorland, with River Cover
SUGGESTED MAP	OS Explorer OL30 Yorkshire Dales – Northern & Central
START/FINISH	Grid reference: SE 047813
DOG FRIENDLINESS	Sheep in fields, so keep dogs on lead
PARKING	Roadside parking below former school in Horsehouse
PUBLIC TOILETS	None en route

It seems hard to believe that the quiet village of Horsehouse was once a place bustling with traffic, as stagecoaches and packhorse trains passed through it on one of the main coaching routes from London to the North. The two inns that existed in the village served the travellers on their way to and from Richmond, one of the region's principal coaching centres. Beyond Horsehouse, to the south-west, Coverdale grows steeper and wilder before the vertiginous descent down Park Rash into Kettlewell in Wharfedale – a journey that must have deeply scared many 17th- and 18th-century travellers. Trains of up to 40 packhorses also used the route, bringing goods to the valley and taking lead and other minerals from the mines on the moors above. Bells jingling on the harness of the leading horse signalled their presence.

Headless Pedlars and a Future King

Pedlars, too, followed the routes, and some met a gruesome end; three headless corpses were found by a side road into Nidderdale. The local constable initiated enquiries and the evidence suggested that they were Scottish pedlars, killed for their money and goods. Their heads were not found – nor were their murderers, though the local finger of suspicion pointed strongly at a Horsehouse innkeeper and her daughter.

West Scrafton, a tiny village set beside Great Gill as it tumbles towards the River Cover below, is dominated by the heights of Great Roova Crags (1549ft/472m). Before the dissolution of the monasteries in the 1530s, the village was owned by the monks of Jervaulx Abbey. Much of the land was subsequently in the hands of the Earl of Lennox – and West Scrafton Manor House is said to have been the birthplace of his son Lord Darnley, murdered second husband of Mary, Queen of Scots and father of King James I and VI. Carlton-in-Coverdale, the next village on the walk is the largest of all the dale's settlements, with some good houses lining the main street and the motte of a small castle visible south of the main street. Flatts Farm at the west end of the village has an inscription to Henry Constantine 'The Coverdale Poet'.

HORSEHOUSE

Miles Coverdale, the first man to translate the whole Bible into English, was born in the valley – no one knows exactly where – in 1488. After some time as a friar in Cambridge, his reforming zeal meant he was forced to live abroad. The first edition of his bible was published in Paris in 1535, and a revised version, known as the Great Bible, in 1538. From 1551 he was Bishop of Exeter, but he was imprisoned under Mary Tudor. In Elizabeth's reign he lived and preached in London until his death in 1568.

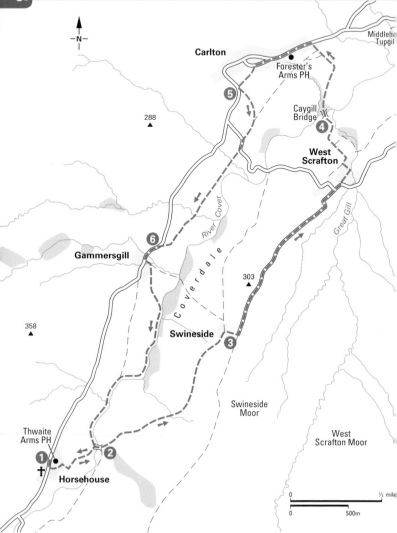

WALK 16 DIRECTIONS

1 Walk past the Thwaite Arms, then curve behind it on a track between houses. Turn right down a signed track through a garden. Go

through two gates, bend left to a third gate, then bear half right to a gate. Continue to a footbridge.

2 Cross the bridge and bear left, uphill. Go over a stile signed

WHILE YOU'RE THERE

Visit the Forbidden Corner, a fantasy garden full of follies, tunnels, secret chambers and passages offering intrigue and unexpected discoveries. Built by a former British Ambassador to Ecuador at Tupgill, 3 miles (4.8km) east of Carlton, the Forbidden Corner is open by timed ticket in advance only – phone 01969 640638 or call in at the tourist information centre in Leyburn.

'Swineside', cross a small field to another stile, then bear half right to go through a small plantation. Keep on in the same direction across open land, crossing a small stream, to a stile, then on to another stile and footpath sign. Bear left across a field to a gap in the left-hand boundary, then contour along a path, which becomes clearer, and cross a stile just above the first building of Swineside Farm.

❸ Follow the track past the farmhouse then right, uphill. At the top, cross a cattle grid and follow the metalled lane for 1.5 miles (2.4km) into West Scrafton. In the village take a track to the left marked as a dead end. Turn left, signed 'Carlton', and follow the walled path round to the right. At its end turn left (footpath sign) down a field. Go through a kissing gate and down to a fingerpost. Turn right down a clear track signed to Caygill Bridge. Follow the field edge to two footbridges.

❹ After the bridges, go through a gate and ascend a steep path into a field. Turn left at a signpost then turn right alongside a wall and on to a gate. Follow a clear path between walls to the road in Carlton. Turn left, passing the Forester's Arms. Where it widens, bear left, then turn left at a footpath sign and cross a stile. Continue straight ahead over stiles to a road.

❺ Turn left and go immediately through a gate. Descend to a stile, bear right to another stile and follow a wall to a stile on to a road. Turn left. At a left bend, go right, over a stile signed 'Gammersgill'. Go over two more stiles and cross a footbridge. Continue ahead to a waymarked gate. Cross the fields, going over a stile and a wooden footbridge, and enter a walled lane. At a sharp right bend, go ahead through a stile, then bear right to a stile on to the road.

WHERE TO EAT AND DRINK

The Thwaite Arms in Horsehouse has a friendly atmosphere but limited hours during the week. The Forester's Arms in Carlton-in-Coverdale is famous for its fine meals and is worth a special journey.

❻ Turn left into Gammersgill, cross the bridge, then turn left though a gate signed 'Swineside'. Bear right to another gate, then cross to a stile beside a gate. Bear half left to the field corner and go over a stile. Now follow the river until you reach the footbridge crossed near the start of the walk. Retrace your steps back to Horsehouse.

WHAT TO LOOK OUT FOR

Like Middleham at the end of the valley, Coverdale is much given over to horses, with riding schools and livery stables throughout the dale. This is not a recent phenomenon – in Daniel Defoe's day the whole area was geared to the horse; in the third volume of his *A Tour through the Whole Island of Great Britain* published in 1726, he wrote that 'all this country is full of jockeys, that is to say, dealers in horses, and breeders of horses…'

Mr Danby's Druidic Dream

A gentle walk from a peculiar mock-druidic temple,
through rich farmland near Masham.

DISTANCE *4.25 miles (6.8km)*   **MINIMUM TIME** *2hrs*

ASCENT/GRADIENT *426ft (130m)* ▲▲▲   **LEVEL OF DIFFICULTY** ✦✦✦

PATHS *Tracks and field paths, 7 stiles*

LANDSCAPE *Valley and farmland, with some surprising constructions*

SUGGESTED MAP *OS Explorer 298 Nidderdale*

START/FINISH *Grid reference: SE 177787*

DOG FRIENDLINESS *Keep dogs on leads or under close control*

PARKING *Car park by Druid's Temple*

PUBLIC TOILETS *None en route*

Start or finish the walk with a druidical flourish by visiting the Druid's Temple – one of the most extraordinary of Yorkshire's rich crop of follies. It was created on the orders of William Danby, eccentric master of nearby Swinton Castle, in 1809. One of his purposes was philanthropy – there was widespread unemployment in Nidderdale, and he saw his version of Stonehenge as an early job creation scheme. What his workers thought when they were paid to build something so strange is not recorded; they were no doubt supposed to remain silent – and grateful.

The Hermit and the Luminous Moss

Danby's Druid's Temple bears only superficial resemblance to Stonehenge. It is oval, not round, and sits in a hollow, solidly lined with great upright stones. At the opposite end from the entrance is a cave, said to contain a rare type of luminous moss. Outside the Temple, like tugs around an ocean liner, are pretend cromlechs, consisting of huge flat stones on uprights. These betray the early 19th-century origins of the temple – they are spaced with perfect symmetry, in the best classical tradition. Less classical, though very fashionable, was the hermit who is said to have inhabited the cave for four and a half years, without cutting his hair or beard.

The walk passes through what was perhaps a trial run for the splendours of the Druid's Temple, a gateway of massively piled boulders, before descending towards the valley of the Pott Beck – a reminder that the area, for council purposes, goes under the delightful name of Ilton-cum-Pott. You will see the dam wall of Leighton Reservoir ahead (you can see the reservoir itself from just beyond the Druid's Temple). It was under construction at the outbreak of the First World War (the neighbouring Roundhill Reservoir had been constructed more than ten years before), and the engineering works were served by a light railway from Masham. As war broke out, the site was taken over by the 1st Leeds Battalion – the Leeds Pals – who were stationed here for nine months, before being transferred first to Ripon, then, via Hampshire and Egypt, to the Somme.

MASHAM

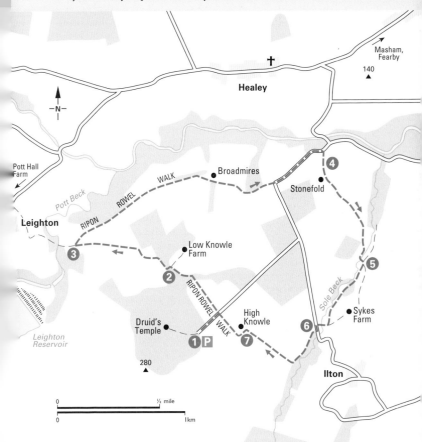

Spurring On

Much of the walk follows the Ripon Rowel Walk, a 50-mile (80km) circular route centred on the city of Ripon, and officially starting from the cathedral. It is, appropriately, named after the rowels – the small spiked wheels fitted to the back of a horserider's spurs – that were Ripon's speciality in the 16th and 17th centuries. So renowned were the rowels manufactured here that a royal charter recognised their superiority, and they gave rise to a common folk saying 'As true steel as Ripon rowels'. A spur appears in the city's coat of arms (along with a horn) and can be seen on the top of the 300-year-old obelisk in the Market Square. Many local clubs and societies also use this symbol in their emblems and even their titles. The Ripon Rowel Walk is well waymarked by a spiked wheel symbol.

WALK 17 DIRECTIONS

❶ Park in the car park by the Druid's Temple (to visit the Temple, walk though the wood, then return to the car park) and walk down the road you drove up. Just after a row of metal posts,

cross a stile on the left marked with the Ripon Rowel Walk symbol, opposite a farm track. Walk ahead across the field and go though a gate surrounded by boulders. Bend left, along the edge of the wood and at the farm track, go left to a gate.

WALK 17

2 After the gate turn right, following the track. It bends away from the wood and down to a ladder stile. After the stile, bear half left across the field towards the pine trees to a stile in a crossing wire fence. Continue ahead, bearing slightly left, to descend by a small wood to two stout wooden posts, one of them waymarked.

3 At the posts turn sharp right, uphill, on the grassy track. Follow the rutted track, mostly level, until it passes to the right of Broadmires farm. The track becomes stony and then leads straight out into a metalled lane. At a road junction continue straight ahead, now descending. On a bend, turn right through a metal gate towards Stonefold farm.

4 Walk past the farmhouse, then turn left through a gate into a small enclosure. Cross a stile and go a few paces to another stile. From this bear right to a gate then continue ahead to a waymarked post. Bear right across the field through a gateway in a crossing

fence and pick up a descending track, which bears right. Below a plantation, leave the track and cross a stile on the left. Follow a narrow path to another stile and a footbridge just beyond.

5 Cross the bridge and go over a waymarked stile, then turn right, along a track. Go through two gates, past a barn, and through another metal gate on to a lane.

6 Turn left, then turn right on the next track. Go over a stile beside a gate, and along the track. After a gateway, turn right alongside a wall, climbing toward the farm on the ridge. Approaching the farm, cross a stile in a wire fence.

7 After the stile, bend to the left, following a wooden fence, in front of the farm building then through a metal gate on your right-hand side. Follow the farm track and exit onto the metalled lane over a stile by the gate. Turn left back to the car park.

Herriot's Darrowby

James Herriot based his fictional
home town on his real one — Thirsk.

DISTANCE	5 miles (8km) MINIMUM TIME 2hrs
ASCENT/GRADIENT	66ft (20m) ▲▲▲ LEVEL OF DIFFICULTY ✦✦✦
PATHS	Town paths, field paths and tracks, 6 stiles
LANDSCAPE	Streamside and undulating pastureland around town
SUGGESTED MAP	OS Explorer 302 Northallerton & Thirsk
START/FINISH	Grid reference: SE 430813
DOG FRIENDLINESS	Keep dogs on lead
PARKING	Roadside parking in the main street of Sowerby village
PUBLIC TOILETS	Thirsk town centre

The elegant Georgian village street of Sowerby – now joined on to the town of Thirsk – is lined with a handsome avenue of lime trees. Such a civilised aspect belies the origins of the village's name, for Sowerby means the 'township in the muddy place'. Once you begin the walk, the reason becomes evident, even in dry weather. Sowerby is on the edge of the flood plain of the Cod Beck. Sowerby Flatts, which you will see across the beck at the start of the walk, and cross at the finish, is a popular venue for impromptu games of soccer and other sports, but is still prone to flooding.

Between Old and New

Once you've crossed the road by the end of New Bridge, you are walking between Old Thirsk and New Thirsk – though new in this context still means medieval. Old Thirsk is set to the east of the Cod Beck; like Sowerby, it too has a watery name, for Thirsk comes from an old Swedish word meaning a 'fen'. New Thirsk, to the west, is centred on the fine cobbled Market Place. The parish church, which you will pass twice, is the best Perpendicular church in North Yorkshire, with a particularly imposing tower.

South Kilvington, at the northern end of the walk, used to be a busy village on the main road north from Thirsk to Yarm. For much of the 19th century it was home to William Kingsley, who was vicar here until his death at the age of 101 in 1916 – having been born as Wellington defeated Napoleon at Waterloo. He entertained both the painter Turner and the art critic John Ruskin here, as well as his cousin Charles Kingsley, author of *The Water Babies*. More than a little eccentric, the vicar had signs in his garden saying 'Beware of Mantraps'. When asked where they were, he paraded his three housemaids.

Darrowby and Wight

For many visitors, the essential place to visit in Thirsk is Skeldale House in Kirkgate – on the right as you return from the church to the Market Square. This was the surgery of local vet James Wight, better known by his pen name, James Herriot. Now an award-winning museum, 'The World of James

THIRSK

Herriot', this was where Wight worked for all his professional life. Thirsk itself is a major character in the books, appearing lightly disguised as Darrowby. The museum has reconstructions of what the surgery and the family rooms were like in the 1940s, and tells the history of veterinary science. Whether or not you're a fan of the Herriot tales, which began with *If Only They Could Talk* in 1970, you'll find it a fascinating and nostalgic tour.

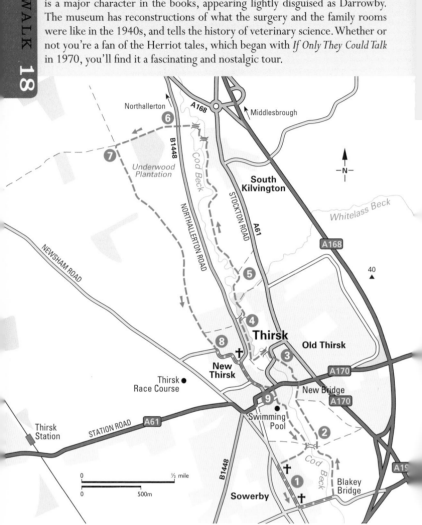

WALK 18 DIRECTIONS

❶ Walk down the village street, away from Thirsk. Just past the Methodist Church on the left, go left down Blakey Lane. Cross the bridge, turn left on a signed path and follow the stream, going through two kissing gates to a footbridge.

❷ Continue beside the stream to a stile. Go through two gates to a car park and ahead to the road. Cross

and take a path that curves left, then right by the bridge. At a paved area, turn right to go alongside a green to a road.

❸ Cross and continue ahead, crossing a main road and going left at the top of the green. Cross the metal bridge and continue beside the beck by the church. Before reaching the road take the path to the right, beside a bench, to a footbridge on the right.

4 Cross the bridge and go straight ahead through two gates, curving left to follow the beck to a gate by a bridge. Go straight ahead (not over the bridge) and follow the path across the fields, veering diagonally right to a stile on your right.

5 Go over the stile and follow the stream, going over another two stiles to pass beside houses. Continue left over a footbridge by some mill buildings. The path winds right to cross a second footbridge. Follow the bridleway sign across the field through a gate to reach the main road.

WHILE YOU'RE THERE

Visit the Thirsk Museum and tourist information centre at 14 Kirkgate. As well as having interesting local exhibits and displays, this was the birthplace, in November 1756, of Thomas Lord. The son of a local farmer, Thomas made his name as a professional cricketer, and set up his own ground in Dorset Square in 1787. Lord's Cricket Ground moved to its present site in 1814.

6 Cross the road and go through a signed gate opposite, to another gate beside a wood. 150 yards (137m) after the wood, turn left at a waymark.

7 Walk down the field with a hedge on your left. In the second

WHERE TO EAT AND DRINK

Thirsk has a good choice of cafés, pubs and hotels. Recommended are the up-market Golden Fleece in the Market Square and the Lord Nelson. Yorks Tea Rooms, nearby, offers good lunches and a range of coffees. In Sowerby, both Sheppard's Hotel and Restaurant and Oswalds offer lunch and dinner.

field, go left over a stile and continue with the hedge on your right, bearing half left to another stile. Continue across the field, then down the next field edge, bearing left, then right at the end to a path that becomes a grassy lane between hedges.

8 At a road go straight ahead, bearing left, then right past the church. Turn right and walk into the town centre. In the Market Square, cross by the clock tower towards the Golden Fleece. Go down a signed passageway two premises to the pub's left, cross a road and go down Villa Place.

9 Bear left to pass the swimming pool. Turn right and bend round the pool building to a gate. Go ahead to a gate and walk parallel with the beck. At the bridge, turn right across the field on a grassy track to a gate on to a lane, turn left, returning back to Sowerby.

WHAT TO LOOK OUT FOR

See if you can catch a film at the Ritz Cinema, just off the Market Square. Built in 1912, it went under several names during its 80-year history, finally closing in 1992 as Studio One. For the previous ten years it had been kept going by a dedicated husband and wife team, but the economics of local cinemas had become almost impossible. The people of Thirsk were determined to have films back in their town, however, and, under the control of Thirsk Town Council, it was reopened in March 1995, reverting to its original name and on a six-month lease. So successful was it, that it still continues to show a regular programme of films. It is now run entirely by volunteers. Its equipment – including a horn-shaped loudspeaker above the screen dating from the 1930s – has been updated, but the Ritz still retains the atmosphere of a typical small-town cinema of the past.

Ingleton and its Falls

*A renowned walk by the falls,
on a route first opened for tourists in 1885.*

DISTANCE 5 miles (8km)   **MINIMUM TIME** 2hrs

ASCENT/GRADIENT 689ft (210m) ▲▲▲   **LEVEL OF DIFFICULTY** +++

PATHS Good paths and tracks, with some steps throughout

LANDSCAPE Two wooded valleys, waterfalls, ancient track, wide views

SUGGESTED MAP OS Explorer OL2 Yorkshire Dales – Southern & Western

START/FINISH Grid reference: SD 693733

DOG FRIENDLINESS Dogs should be on leads by waterfalls

PARKING Pay-and-display car park in centre of Ingleton, or at start of Waterfalls Walk

PUBLIC TOILETS Ingleton

NOTE Steep admission charge for Waterfalls Walk

This is one of the classic walks of the Yorkshire Dales, and was first opened to visitors in 1885. A workaday town, and today one of the Dales' honeypots, Ingleton shows its mining and quarrying history in its buildings. It became a place for tourists to visit when the railway arrived in 1859 – the viaduct almost cuts the village in half. The entrepreneurs who developed the Waterfalls Walk in the 1880s, and charged for the privilege of taking the route, were tapping into the start of one of the most profitable of industries in the Dales.

Cascades and Strata

The spectacle of the Waterfalls Walk begins in Swilla Glen, where the River Twiss passes through a deep gorge, with rapids and whirlpools giving a taste of what is to come. The first of the cascades soon follows – Pecca Falls, where the river tumbles over a shelf of the hard greywacke stone, eating away at the softer slate beds below. Beyond, the narrow glen opens out as you approach Thornton Force. Unlike the other falls on the walk, this is not a series of rapids confined within the valley, but a majestic plunge of water 40ft (12m) from its lip of hard limestone into a pool gouged into the slate beds below, which have been heaved into a vertical position. This is one of the classic spots for studying the geology of the area; the different strata are conveniently exposed. A glacier came to this part of the valley – the tip of its nose reached just above the point where the water now falls. Here it deposited the mass of boulder-clay it had pushed in front of it; the remains can still be made out beside the fall.

Limestone and Water

The route beyond follows Twisleton Lane, an ancient packhorse route on the line of the Roman road from Bainbridge to Ingleton. Above you are Twisleton Scars, great bands of limestone interspersed with horizontal bands of shale. One of the best limestone pavements in the area is to be found at the top of the Scars. The walk then joins the second of the waterfall-filled valleys, this time of the River Doe, on its way back to Ingleton. The woodland here is some of the oldest and most unspoiled in the area, with ancient oak trees flanking the waterfalls. Eventually the route leaves the river and comes out into a former limestone quarry – there is still quarrying in the area, for the greywacke, which is used for road surfacing. Ingleton also once supported a number of cotton mills, powered by water diverted in mill races from the rivers.

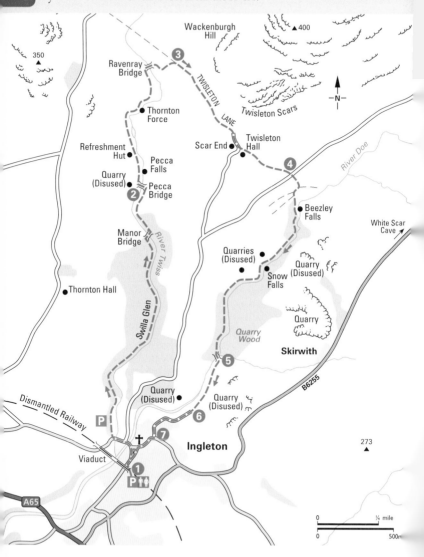

WALK 19 DIRECTIONS

❶ Leave the car park in the centre of Ingleton at its western end. Turn right along the road and follow the

'Waterfalls Walk' signs, which take you downhill and across the river to the entrance to the falls. Pay the admission fee, walk through the car park, and go through a kissing

INGLETON

gate. The path undulates, with steps in places. Cross Manor Bridge and continue upstream, now with the river on your left, to Pecca Bridge.

2 Cross the bridge and turn right, continuing upstream and climbing to pass a refreshment hut before reaching Thornton Force. The path winds slightly away from the stream and up steps to pass the waterfall, and then takes you over Ravenray Bridge, and up more steps, to a kissing gate on to Twisleton Lane.

3 Turn right along the rough lane, where there's often an ice cream van. The track descends to a farmyard. Keep following 'Waterfalls Walk' signs through here, over a gated stone stile. Continue along the track, then though a kissing gate and on to a road.

4 Go straight across the road. The track soon bends right, passing a house. Go through a gate, then another into woodland. The path passes Beezley Falls and Rival Falls. A little further down, a side-path to the left leads to a footbridge with a good view of the deep and narrow Baxenghyll Gorge. Continue down the main path, which takes you to another footbridge.

5 Cross the bridge, then follow the path past old slate workings,

then away from the water into trees below the present-day quarry. The path eventually passes through the old limestone quarry workings. Continue through a hand gate on to a lane.

6 Beyond the gate follow the lane, soon entering Ingleton.

7 Reaching a T-junction in the centre of the village, go right and follow the road round. Just before the railway viaduct, steps on the left lead back up to the car park.

Erratic Progress

*From Austwick along ancient tracks
to see the famous Norber Erratics.*

DISTANCE *5.5 miles (8.8km)*   MINIMUM TIME *2hrs 30min*

ASCENT/GRADIENT *558ft (170m)* ▲▲▲   LEVEL OF DIFFICULTY +++

PATHS *Field and moorland paths, tracks, lanes on return, 10 stiles*

LANDSCAPE *Farmland and limestone upland*

SUGGESTED MAP *OS Explorer OL2 Yorkshire Dales – Southern & Western*

START/FINISH *Grid reference: SD 769683*

DOG FRIENDLINESS *Dogs should be on leads*

PARKING *Roadside parking near Austwick Bridge, and in village*

PUBLIC TOILETS *None en route*

There is nothing showy about Austwick village. A pleasant, grey-built village, it has several old cottages, many of them dated in the traditional Dales way by a decorative lintel above the main door, showing the initials of the couple who had it built, together with the year they moved in. They mostly date from around the end of the 17th century. On the green in the centre is the restored market cross. The market itself, lost centuries ago to nearby Clapham, has not been restored.

Robin Proctor and Nappa

The walk takes you up Town Head Lane from the village, and across fields into Thwaite Lane. To your left is the ridge of limestone called Robin Proctor's Scar, named after a local farmer whose horse was trained to bring him home after a long night spent in the local pub. One night, too drunk to tell, he mounted the wrong horse, and it plunged over the crag with the farmer on its back. The area below the scar was formerly a tarn, and is now home to a wide variety of marsh plants. Nappa Scar, which the walk passes after you have visited the Norber Erratics, is on the North Craven Fault line. The path goes along a ledge below a steep cliff. In the cliff wall you can see the different strata of rock, including mixed conglomerate and limestone.

The Norber Erratics are world-famous. To geologists they are a place of pilgrimage, and even the non-specialist can tell that something odd is going on here. When you arrive on the plateau above Nappa Scar, you find an extensive grass-covered area, with the remnants of a limestone pavement poking through the tufts. Strewn all over the pavement are grey boulders, some of them of huge size, perched on limestone plinths. These are the erratics. Blocks of ancient greywacke stone, they were carried here from Crummackdale, more than 0.5 mile (800m) away, by the power of a glacier, and dumped when the ice retreated. Over the centuries, the elements have worn down the limestone pavement on which they stand – except where the erratics protected it, resulting in their elevated position.

AUSTWICK

After you cross Crummack Lane and walk though fields with a limestone ridge and ancient agricultural enclosures, you will reach Austwick Beck, where the water is crossed by an ancient clapper bridge – flat stones laid across the stream from bank to bank. This leads into a walled track that takes you to the hamlet of Wharfe. The route returns to Austwick along other walled lanes. These are the remains of old monastic ways that linked the granges, high on the fells, to the monasteries like Fountains Abbey which owned the vast sheep walks.

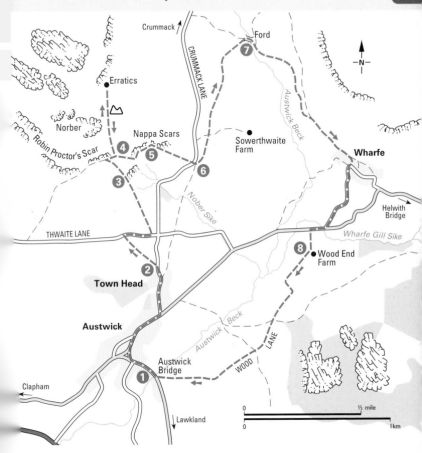

WALK 20 DIRECTIONS

❶ From your parking place near the bridge, walk through the village. Bear right at the triangular green, following the signpost to Horton in Ribblesdale. Pass the Gamecock Inn and, just past a cottage called Hobbs Gate, turn left up Town Head Lane. Just above the last of the houses, go left over a waymarked ladder stile.

❷ Walk up the field to another stile, and on to another stile on to a lane. Turn right. Just before reaching a metalled road, turn left over a ladder stile and follow a track. As the track veers left, go straight on, following the stone wall to a stone stile by a gate.

❸ Cross the stile and continue up beside the wall. Where this bends left, by a very large boulder across

WHILE YOU'RE THERE

Clapham village, which stole Austwick's market, has a beck flowing through its centre, and is surrounded by attractive woodland. The village blacksmith at the end of the 18th century was James Faraday, father of the scientist Michael Faraday. From here, too, came the botanist Reginald Farrer, whose name appears in the Latin names of many of the plant species he discovered.

the path, go right on a track to pass the right-hand edge of the scar. When you reach a signpost, go up left, signposted 'Norber'.

④ Follow the path up on to the plateau, and explore the Norber Erratics. Return the same way, back to the signpost. Turn left, following the sign for Crummack. Follow the green path downhill then back up beside a wall by the scar to a stone stile on your right.

⑤ Descend to a gap by another stile and follow the path beneath a rocky outcrop. Continue downhill, with a wall on your left, to reach a ladder stile on to a metalled lane. Cross the lane and go over another ladder stile opposite.

⑥ Turn left across the field. Go over two ladder stiles, cross a farm track and go straight ahead

over a rocky ridge to a stone stile. Continue to a gated stile, go left a few paces and then turn right on a track. This soon leads to a ford and clapper bridge.

⑦ Follow the track between the walls for 0.5 mile (800m) into Wharfe. Turn left at a T-junction in the hamlet, then follow the road round to the right and go down the village approach road to reach a metalled road. Turn right. After 100yds (91m), turn left at a bridleway sign to Feizor, down the road to Wood End Farm.

WHERE TO EAT AND DRINK

The Game Cock Inn in Austwick is a traditional village pub with good ale and food. On the main A65 road just outside the village is the Cross Streets Inn, which has meals at lunchtimes and in the evening. Very much up-market is the Austwick Traddock, close to the start of the walk: fine dining is the name of the game here.

⑧ Turn right on a track beside the entrance to the farmyard. Follow it as it bends left and right, then bear right where another track joins from the left. Reaching a crossroads of tracks, go straight ahead, following the line of telegraph poles. The track winds to reach the metalled lane into the village, a few paces from the bridge.

WHAT TO LOOK OUT FOR

Nothing is as characteristic of the Yorkshire Dales as its limestone scenery. It is technically known to geologists as a karst landscape – one that has underground drainage, with sinkholes and caves, dry valleys and limestone pavements like those above Crummackdale. Unlike most rocks, limestone is a soluble stone that is constantly being cleaned by the action of rainfall. Soils are not formed, plants do not appear, and the limestone remains pristine in its whiteness. But it is certainly not an unchanging landscape. The glaciers which originally scraped clean the limestone pavements have left their mark elsewhere, in the deep-gouged valleys and in the clefts in the landscape where their melt waters have torn through the rock. Even more spectacular are the caves under your feet, and the mysterious entrances to them. As you walk through this landscape, stalagmites and stalactites are still being formed beneath your feet.

Forces of Nature at Catrigg and Stainforth

From an attractive, stone-built village in the heart of the Ribble Valley, with a visit to two impressive waterfalls.

DISTANCE 4.75 miles (7.7km)   **MINIMUM TIME** 2hrs

ASCENT/GRADIENT 525ft (160m) ▲▲▲   **LEVEL OF DIFFICULTY** ✦✦✦

PATHS Green lanes, field and riverside paths, some road, 8 stiles

LANDSCAPE Moorland, farmland and river meadows with two waterfalls

SUGGESTED MAP OS Explorer OL2 Yorkshire Dales – Southern & Western

START/FINISH Grid reference: SD 821672

DOG FRIENDLINESS Can be off lead in walled section up to Catrigg Force

PARKING Pay-and-display car park in Stainforth, just off B6479

PUBLIC TOILETS At car park

Stainforth is set along the Stainforth Beck as it rushes to join the River Ribble. It provides the starting point for many tracks across the moors to the east, once important routes for trade, that crossed the beck at first on the stone ford (which is what 'Stainforth' means) and later by the 14th-century bridge. The walk follows one of these ancient ways, the walled Goat Lane, as far as the path down to Catrigg Force. This spectacular waterfall, hidden in a wooded valley, was one of the favourite places of the composer Edward Elgar, who regularly stayed with his friend Dr Charles Buck in nearby Settle. Elgar would walk here, perhaps mulling over his latest work as he did so. Towards the end of the walk you pass another waterfall, Stainforth Force, where the Ribble passes over a series of limestone steps in tumultuous cascades. Just above is an attractive humpback bridge leading to Little Stainforth. The bridge was a vital link on a packhorse route between Lancaster and Ripon.

Saving the Pavement

After Catrigg Force, the walk route winds, after superb views towards Fountains Fell, towards the farms at Winskill. On the moorland just above are the Winskill Stones, pedestals of limestone topped with slate deposited here by ice age glaciers. The slate protected the limestone beneath from the erosion that has worn down the surrounding rock. An area of limestone pavement here is now a nature reserve, but was for many years quarried for ornamental garden rocks. After a campaign to prevent this destruction, 64 acres (26ha) was purchased from the owner for £200,000. Now the area, with its rare limestone plants, is preserved; it is dedicated to the memory of television gardener Geoff Hamilton, who was patron of the appeal that raised the funds to buy the land.

Sir Isaac Newton often came to Langcliffe Hall, which has an odd door surround probably carved by the same masons who worked on the much more elaborate house in Settle known as The Folly. Newton was friendly with the local landowners, the Paleys. One of the family, William Paley, wrote a famous book, *Evidences of Christianity* (1794). Also in Langcliffe is a

STAINFORTH

former inn called the Naked Woman – a counterpart of the better-known Naked Man in Settle. If you're lucky enough to be in Langcliffe during a wedding, linger for a while to see an old Dales custom; while the ceremony takes place in the church, the village children tie up the churchyard gates and refuse to let the newly-married couple out until the guests have thrown money to them.

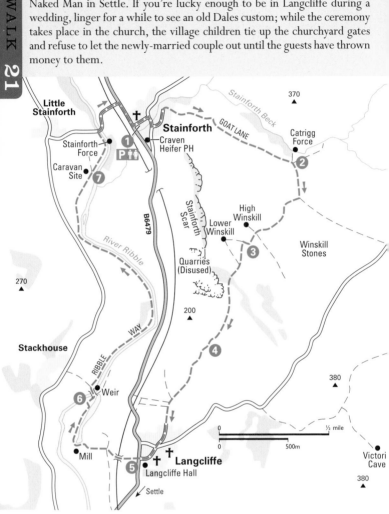

WALK 21 DIRECTIONS

❶ From the car park turn right, then right again, signed 'Settle'. Over the bridge, go immediately left through a gap in the wall. Follow the narrow path to an open area. Go through white posts and turn left. Keep right of the green, then turn right. Follow the track uphill for 0.75 mile (1.2km) to a gate. (To visit Catrigg Force, take a smaller gate to the left, then go left again. Return to the same point.)

❷ After the gate, the track bends right. Go through another gate, then turn right, signed 'Winskill'. Join a track which bears left and runs between walls. At a signpost near the farmhouses, go straight ahead over a cattle grid and down a track signed 'Stainforth and Langcliffe'. Just after a right-hand bend, go left over a stile signed 'Langcliffe'.

❸ Cross the field to a gate and stile, turning right immediately

STAINFORTH

⑥ Go through the gate and turn right between the rows of cottages. Where the row ends, go left over a footbridge over the River Ribble and at the end turn right to a stone stile beside the weir, signed 'Stainforth'. Follow the riverside path 0.75 mile (1.2km) before steps lead to a stile and an elevated stretch. The path returns gradually to the river side and approaches a caravan site.

afterwards. The path soon descends steeply to a hand gate, bearing left just below to traverse the slope before descending to a gate. Follow the track beyond to another gate.

④ The track, now walled, leads into Langcliffe village. At a crossroads of tracks go a couple of paces right, then left (almost straight on). At the main street bear right, then keep straight on to reach the main road.

⑤ Cross the road to a gap in the wall diagonally right. Follow the footpath over a railway footbridge. Follow a lane ('No Entry' sign) towards a mill. Signs, barriers and fences guide the path round the works to emerge beside the millpond. Follow the pond-side path to reach a gate on the left by houses.

⑦ Go right of the site, on the riverside path, past Stainforth Force to the humpback Stainforth Bridge. Go through a stile on to the lane, turn right over the bridge and follow the narrow lane as it bends and climbs to the main road. Turn right and take the second turning left back to the car park.

Over from Littondale

From unspoiled Arncliffe to Kettlewell,
and back by the River Skirfare.

WALK 22

DISTANCE 6.5 miles (10.4km)   **MINIMUM TIME** 3hrs 30min

ASCENT/GRADIENT 1,315ft (400m) ▲▲▲   **LEVEL OF DIFFICULTY** +++

PATHS Mostly clear, some rocky sections; may be muddy, 16 stiles

LANDSCAPE Rocky hillside, moorland and meadows

SUGGESTED MAP OS Explorer OL30 Yorkshire Dales – Northern & Central

START/FINISH Grid reference: SD 932719

DOG FRIENDLINESS On leads – sheep in fields and on moorland

PARKING In Arncliffe, near church

PUBLIC TOILETS In Kettlewell (just off route)

The village of Arncliffe may look familiar to long-time *Emmerdale* fans, for the opening titles for many years featured views of the village, and in the programme's very early days it was used as a film location. The cameras have long departed, leaving visitors space to appreciate Arncliffe's spectacular setting. Great limestone scars – once the home to eagles who gave the village its name – line the hillsides all around, and the fells are riddled with caves and gulleys. Arncliffe sits on a great spit of gravel, above the floodplain of the River Skirfare. Before the building of the bridge, a ford allowed travellers an easy crossing for the many ancient tracks that converge here. Some of the tracks may be prehistoric; there is evidence south of the village of Celtic field systems and stone enclosures.

Flodden and a Challenging Cleric

St Oswald's Church may have been Saxon in origin, but nothing remains of that or its Norman successor. The tower is 15th-century, while the rest was rebuilt in both the 18th and 19th centuries. The village records stretch back a long way however; the church retains a list of 34 men from the parish who went north from here in 1513 to fight the Scots at the Battle of Flodden. In the churchyard is a simple stone memorial to John Robinson, Bishop of Woolwich, who caused a theological stir with his book *Honest to God*, published in 1963. In Bridge House, close by, Charles Kingsley wrote part of *The Water Babies* – his Vendale is Littondale. Arncliffe's houses, built of local stone, are set informally around the church and the green. There is some suggestion that it may have been initially a planned village, set here by monks who were clearing people off the surrounding land so that farming could be carried out more profitably.

Leaving Arncliffe, you will almost immediately begin the long climb up the hillside to Park Scar. The path passes through a patch of ancient woodland, Byre Bank Wood, which has regenerated itself with little management or felling for centuries, because of its precarious foothold on a steep bank. There are rare plants and flowers to be found among the trees. The descent to Kettlewell takes you through The Slit, a narrow cleft in the limestone rocks above the village, while approach to Hawkswick gives views over Littondale, much of which

ARNCLIFFE

is a conservation area. The fields are managed as wildflower meadows that provide winter fodder for the cattle. Littondale is also a must for ornithologists – look out for curlews, peregrine falcons and redshanks, as well as dippers, oystercatchers and yellow wagtails.

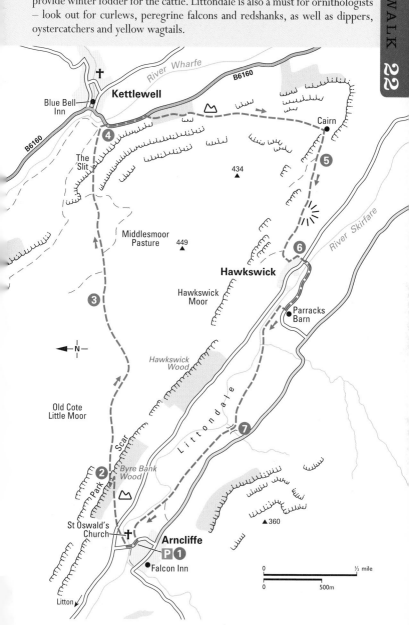

WALK 22 DIRECTIONS

1 From the car park, cross the bridge and turn immediately right, over a gated stile. Walk parallel with the river, cross the road via two stiles, then bear right and follow the footpath uphill over a stile and through a gate. Continue up in the same direction through the woods of Park Scar, with one short zig-zag near the top, to a stile.

Overleaf: Distant view of the village of Kettlewell (Walk 22)

② Bear right and follow the footpath to another stile. Keep on the same heading to pass a signpost, a tumbled wall and then another signpost. The path bears left, crosses a line of shakeholes and continues via a stile to another stile on the ridge.

③ Descend on the same heading. The path passes more shakeholes and descends beside a wall to a ladder stile. Follow the path down, descending steeply to a signpost. Cross a track and reach another signpost above a limestone scar overlooking Kettlewell. Descend a narrow cleft (The Slit), then descend to a track. Turn right and walk to the road.

④ Turn right for 300yds (274m), then go right through a gate by a fingerpost, bearing right again at another sign. Climb through woodland, go through a gate, then bear right and up to a small ruin. Continue along the edge of trees and round to a gateway beside a stile. Bear left to another stile then ascend the grassy path, keeping right where it forks, along a broad shelf. Eventually reach another stile

WHERE TO EAT AND DRINK

The Falcon Inn in Arncliffe has been run by the same family for four generations. Here you'll be served good beer direct from the barrel. There are no pumps, pot jugs are filled at the barrel and the ale is poured from them into your glass. They also serve home-cooked food – but prefer notice of vegetarian diners!

WHILE YOU'RE THERE

The village of Litton is further up Littondale where the valley narrows, while beyond is the hamlet of Halton Gill. An 18th-century curate here, the Revd Miles Wilson, wrote a book to explain astronomy to ordinary folk. In *The Man in the Moon*, he imagines a cobbler climbing to the moon from the top of Pen-y-ghent, then wandering around the solar system.

and begin to descend, bending right by a cairn.

⑤ At a track junction continue ahead, with a wall on your left. The track leads down into Hawkswick village. On the outskirts go left, curve right between buildings and descend to the lane.

⑥ Cross the bridge and follow the lane round right. Just before farm buildings on the left, turn right towards a footbridge; turn left before it at the 'Arncliffe' sign. Follow the river to a footbridge over a side-stream and continue to a double gate. The path bears slightly away from the river to a gate. Cross the field beyond, skirting a steep bank above the river, to another footbridge.

⑦ Walk past a barn and through a gate, then bear left to a squeeze stile and cross a track. From the next stile bear slightly right to rejoin the river. Follow the path, with plentiful waymarks and signs, to emerge by the churchyard and return to the starting point.

WHAT TO LOOK OUT FOR

The ancient village of Kettlewell's name means the stream in a narrow valley – the village is built alongside the Dowber Gill Beck as it tumbles into the River Wharfe. Towering over Kettlewell are the long ridges of limestone and the huge bulk of Great Whernside. A weekly market used to be held at Kettlewell, which was on one of the main coaching routes from London to the North – beyond the village the route went over into Coverdale and into Richmond.

Scar House and Nidderdale

A walk in Upper Nidderdale,
with natural and artificial landscapes.

DISTANCE *8.5 miles (13.7km)*   MINIMUM TIME *3hrs 45min*

ASCENT/GRADIENT *1050ft (320m)* ▲▲▲   LEVEL OF DIFFICULTY +++

PATHS *Moorland tracks, field paths and lanes, 11 stiles*

LANDSCAPE *High hills of Upper Nidderdale, farmland and riverside*

SUGGESTED MAP *OS Explorer 298 Nidderdale or OS Explorer OL30 Yorkshire Dales – Northern & Central*

START/FINISH *Grid reference: SE 070766*

DOG FRIENDLINESS *Can be off leads on moorland, on lead in farmland*

PARKING *Signed car park at top of reservoir access road*

PUBLIC TOILETS *By car park*

Opened in 1936, Scar House is one of a string of reservoirs in Nidderdale that serve the city of Bradford, 30 miles (48km) to the south – the others include Angram, to the west, and Gouthwaite, down the valley towards Pateley Bridge. It is still possible to see evidence around the dam of the remains of the village in which the navvies who built it lived and of the ancillary buildings where they stored machinery and dressed the stone. There were some protests before the dams were built about the drowning of parts of the valley, and rumours that Nidderdale was left out of the Yorkshire Dales National Park when it was designated in 1954 because the reservoirs had blighted the landscape. Redress was made in 1994 when 603 square miles (1562 sq km) of Nidderdale became an Area of Outstanding Natural Beauty.

How Stean Gorge

'Yorkshire's Little Switzerland' says the publicity for How Stean Gorge. The How Stean Beck has forced its way through the limestone here, cutting a gorge up to 80ft (25m) deep, with pools and overhangs enough to please both geologists and small children. Lichen and moss cling to the rock walls, and trees overhang it precariously. For a fee, you can enter the gorge, crossing and re-crossing by footbridges and exploring the narrow paths. The more adventurous can borrow a torch to investigate the deep Tom Taylor's Cave, said to be named after a highwayman who holed up here.

The village of Middlesmoor, visible after passing How Stean Gorge, is one of the most dramatically-sited in the area. Set high on a bluff of the hills overlooking the Nidd Valley, its 19th-century church is on the site of a building thought to have been founded by St Chad. One of the most notorious of Victorian murderers, Eugene Aram, who killed his wife's lover and was hanged when the body came to light 14 years later, was married here. Following the Nidderdale Way from Lofthouse, you may well see groups donning caving gear. They are likely to be preparing to enter the Goyden Pot system, 3.5 miles (5.7km) of underground caves and passages cut through the limestone by the River Nidd. An early guide book noted that 'Goyden

UPPER NIDDERDALE

Pot Hole is a large Rock, into which the River Nidd enters by an arch finely formed… with a lighted candle a person may walk three hundred yards into it with safety.' This procedure is not recommended today!

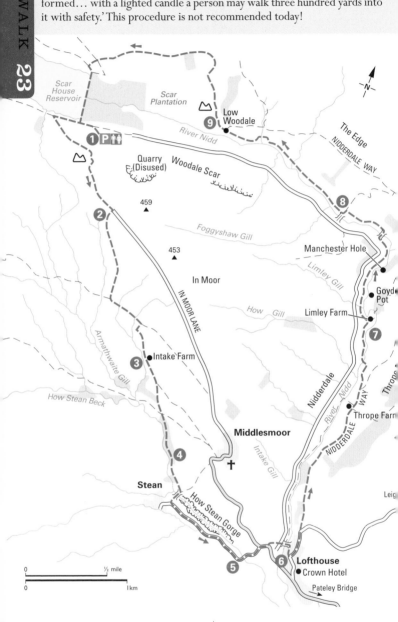

WALK 23 DIRECTIONS

1 Walk past the dam and along the side of the reservoir to a Nidderdale Way signpost. Turn sharp left. The stony track climbs below crags then zig-zags up to open moor. Continue to a gate. A few paces beyond, go right through another gate.

2 Follow a path down to a wall and bear left. Follow sheep-tracks through thick heather, roughly

UPPER NIDDERDALE

parallel to the wall, to a track. Turn left and cross two cattle-grids. Turn right, down to a gate. Walk down the field to a gate just right of a house.

❸ Descend to a gate left of a ruined barn. Bear right through a gateway then bear left to pass right of another barn. Continue in the same direction into woodland. A clearer path joins from the right; continue ahead, slanting down to the riverside.

❹ Follow the path above the river, then through a field to a limekiln. Bear left to a ladder stile then follow the edge of woodland to a gate and Nidderdale Way sign. Turn right down steps to cross a footbridge over the river. Follow the path to a lane and go left, passing How Stean Gorge entrance, to a stone bridge.

❺ Follow the lane over the bridge to a T-junction and turn right. At a layby on a bend go through a kissing gate. Follow the path beside a cricket ground. Cross a lane and go over a bridge. Bear right and pass between buildings into Lofthouse.

❻ Turn left uphill. As the road bends right, go left on a level grassy track. Ignore branches to the right and follow the main track to Thrope Farm. Keep straight ahead until a waymarked sunken path slants down to the river. Walk upstream then cross to a waymarked gate. Follow a path above the river then join a track towards a farm.

❼ Pass metal sheds, then bear left to a gate beside a house. Follow the track to the riverbank and continue upstream, passing Goyden Pot (obvious) and Manchester Hole (in the far bank). Eventually you reach a footbridge over the river. Cross, turn left and continue along the riverside. At New Houses go through a gate, cross a lane and continue along the riverside track.

❽ Where the track bends right, go ahead through stone stiles and continue to a wooden stile. Climb slightly, then bear left to a gate. Descend to another gate, then bear right to a farm. Go ahead between the buildings to a track which climbs and bends right to pass another house.

❾ Climb to a gap between high walls. Continue uphill with a broken wall on your right, to a gate. Go half left through bracken, to a clear track. Turn left, passing a plantation, and follow the track until it crosses another track, directly above the dam. Descend to the dam and cross back to the car park.

Overleaf: A bridge over the narrow river running through the How Stean Gorge in Nidderdale (Walk 23)

Spectacular Landscapes in Limestone Country

The noble Malham Cove is the majestic highlight of this quintessential limestone Dales walk.

DISTANCE 6.25 miles (10.1km)   **MINIMUM TIME** 3hrs

ASCENT/GRADIENT 1,148ft (350m) ▲▲▲   **LEVEL OF DIFFICULTY** +++

PATHS Well-marked field and moorland paths, more than 400 steps in descent from Malham Cove, 5 stiles

LANDSCAPE Spectacular limestone country, including Malham Cove

SUGGESTED MAP OS Explorer OL2 Yorkshire Dales – Southern & Western

START/FINISH Grid reference: SD 894658

DOG FRIENDLINESS Mostly off lead, except where sheep are present or signs indicate otherwise

PARKING At Water Sinks, near gateway across road

PUBLIC TOILETS Car park in Malham village

As you begin this walk, the stream from Malham Tarn suddenly disappears in a tumble of rocks. This is the aptly-named Water Sinks. In spectacular limestone country like this, it is not unusual for streams to plunge underground – it was subterranean watercourses that sculpted the cave systems beneath your feet. As you will see as you continue, this particular stream has not always been so secretive. The now-dry valley of Watlowes just beyond Water Sinks was formed by water action. It was this stream, in fact, that produced Malham Cove, and once fell over its spectacular cliff in a waterfall 230ft (70m) high. Although in very wet weather the stream goes a little further than Water Sinks, it is 200 years since water reached the cove.

Pavement and Cove

Beyond Watlowes valley you reach a stretch of limestone pavement – not the biggest, but probably the best-known example of this unusual phenomenon in the Dales. The natural fissures in the rock have been enlarged by millennia of rain and frost, forming the characteristic blocks, called clints, and the deep clefts, called grikes. Look closely into the grikes; their sheltered environment provides a home to spleenworts and ferns, and sometimes rare primulas. The limestone pavement is the summit of the most spectacular of natural features in the Yorkshire Dales – the huge sweep of the cliffs known as Malham Cove. Take care as you explore the pavement, as the edge is not fenced. As you descend the 400-plus steps, the sheer scale of the Cove becomes apparent. It was formed by a combination of earth movement (it is on the line of the Middle Craven Fault), glacial action and the biting away of its lip by the former waterfall.

Fields, Falls and Fairies

On the slopes to the east of Malham Cove you can see ancient terraced fields. Up to 200yds (183m) long, they were painstakingly cut and levelled

MALHAM

by Anglian farmers in the 8th century for producing crops. They show
how the population was expanding then – there was simply not enough
farmland on the valley floors to feed everyone. Beyond Malham village, the
route passes through fields and a wooded gorge – called Little Gordale – to
Janet's Foss. One of the classic waterfalls of the Dales, it is noted for the
screen of tufa, a soft, porous limestone curtain formed by deposits from
the stream, that now lies over the original lip of stone that was responsible
for creating the fall. Janet (or Jennett) was the Queen of the local fairies,
and is said to have lived in the cave behind the fall.

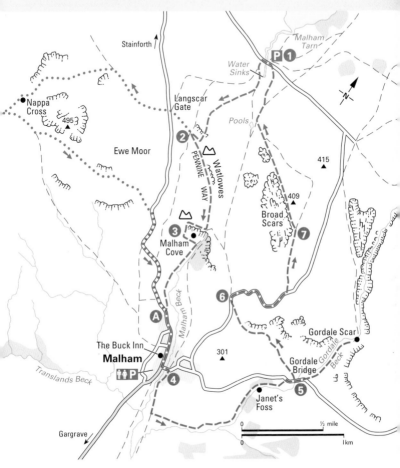

WALK 24 DIRECTIONS

❶ From the car parking space,
walk through the gate, then turn
left through the kissing gate at the
Malham Cove sign. Keep left at
the next signpost, following the
Pennine Way down the dry valley
until the path bends sharp right,
overlooking another dry valley.

❷ Turn left, cross a stile and
descend steeply into the lower
valley. Walk down the level valley
to a stile at the end. Just beyond
this is the limestone pavement
at the top of Malham Cove.
Turn right and walk along the
pavement. Take great care here,
both of the sheer drop down
to your left and the gaps in the

limestone pavement (known as grikes). Turn left to descend beside a stone wall; go through a gate, then descend more than 400 steps to the foot of the Cove.

❸ At the bottom fork left to visit the very base of the cliff, then follow the obvious track beside the river. On reaching the road, turn left and follow it into the centre of Malham village. Turn left to cross the bridge.

❹ Turn immediately right on a track past some houses, then continue along a gravelled path. Follow it left at a sign to Janet's Foss. Eventually the footpath enters woodland, then climbs beside a waterfall (Janet's Foss) to a kissing gate. Turn right along the road, towards Gordale Scar.

WHERE TO EAT AND DRINK

As one of the most visited villages of the Yorkshire Dales, Malham is well-supplied with eating places. Beck Hall Café, the first you come to, has a riverside garden. The Buck Inn has good pub meals and fine beer. The Lister Arms Hotel provides good food, real ale and, in summer, real cider.

---

❺ At Gordale Bridge (actually two bridges), go through a gate to the left. (To visit Gordale Scar, continue straight ahead here. Take a signed gate to the left and follow the path through a field into the gorge. Continue as far as the

---

WHILE YOU'RE THERE

Visit Gordale Scar (a short walk beyond Janet's Foss). The route takes you along a valley that rapidly narrows and twists beneath overhanging rocks, until a final bend brings you to the waterfall in the narrowest part of the gorge. Once thought to be a collapsed cave system, it is now believed to have been formed by erosion from the stream, which has carved this spectacular gash through the limestone.

---

waterfall and then follow the same route back to the bridge.) On the main route, follow the signed public footpath uphill through three gates. Climb alongside a lane before emerging onto it.

❻ Turn right and follow the lane uphill for 600yds (549m), to a ladder stile on the left. Follow a track to a footpath fingerpost.

❼ Bear left and walk over a broad open moor before descending to some small pools. Turn right at a sign for Malham Tarn, go over a ladder stile, take the left-hand path and follow it back to the car park.

EXTENDING THE WALK

You can avoid the steep descent by Malham Cove by taking a scenic extension to this walk, across the limestone uplands to Nappa Cross and descending to Malham along an old drove road which joins a minor road to rejoin the main route at Point ❹.

WHAT TO LOOK OUT FOR

Nothing is what is seems in the Alice-in-Wonderland world around Malham. The logical among us would assume that if water disappears underground, heading in the direction of Malham Cove, just a mile (1.6km) ahead, it will reappear at the base of the Cove. But logic is wrong. The stream that bubbles up from under Malham Cove actually comes from Smelt Mill Sink, 0.75 mile (1.2km) to the west of Water Sinks. The stream from Water Sinks, on the other hand, reappears at Aire Head Springs to become the infant River Aire.

The Monks' Road and Bordley

Remote farmsteads and an old walled green lane between Malhamdale and Wharfedale.

DISTANCE	5 miles (8km) MINIMUM TIME 2hrs
ASCENT/GRADIENT	436ft (133m) ▲▲▲ LEVEL OF DIFFICULTY ✦✦✦
PATHS	Tracks and field paths, 2 stiles
LANDSCAPE	Moorland and farmland
SUGGESTED MAP	OS Explorer OL2 Yorkshire Dales – Southern & Western
START/FINISH	Grid reference: SD 952653
DOG FRIENDLINESS	On leads – sheep on moorland and livestock in fields
PARKING	Roadside parking, where lane reaches open moor
PUBLIC TOILETS	None en route

Many places in the Yorkshire Dales can be described as 'remote' – and Bordley must be one of the least accessible. No metalled roads lead to it, and the settlement (really only a hamlet of a couple of farmhouses) is almost invisible from most of the surrounding countryside, lying as it does in a secluded hollow of the hills. Although the buildings are mostly 18th and 19th century, Bordley has a long, if uneventful, history. It is mentioned in Domesday Book as Borelaie, and its Old English name may mean 'the wood from which the boards were taken' – or perhaps 'the woodland clearing belonging to Brorda'. Whichever it is, the woods have long since gone, and this is now moorland country, some of it enclosed and improved in the 18th century for agriculture. Around Bordley there is evidence of an even older settlement. Mastiles Lane ploughs through the middle of a Roman camp a little way to the west, while to the east, just off the road up from Skirethorns, is evidence of a prehistoric field system.

Mastiles and the Monks

The early part of the walk takes you to Mastiles Gate, one of the landmarks along Mastiles Lane, a superb green track that for centuries has linked Wharfedale and Malhamdale. Its origins were monastic; the monks of Fountains Abbey near Ripon needed straightforward access to their vast estates in the southern parts of the Yorkshire Dales and in the Lake District. So, like the Romans before them, they constructed long roads directly over the fells. The route over Kilnsey Moor was marked by crosses – the bases of some survive along the route. The monastic route crossed the River Wharfe by a wooden bridge at Kilnsey, and then went on to Ripon along the route of what is now the B6265 via Pateley Bridge.

In the 18th and 19th centuries Mastiles Lane was used as a drove road, when great herds of cattle were driven along the lane to market. There was a regular sale at Great Close, near Malham Tarn, where up to 5,000 cattle, most of them from Scotland, were regularly sold. It was at this time that the lane received its walls, to prevent the cattle straying.

Tarmac Outcry

In the early 1960s plans were put forward to tarmac Mastiles Lane so that traffic would be able to drive from Malham into Wharfedale. A public outcry quickly saw the idea abandoned and the route is still a haven of peace for walkers and riders – though more recently there has been further controversy, this time about the use of such green lanes by four-wheel drive off-road vehicles, which can cause damage.

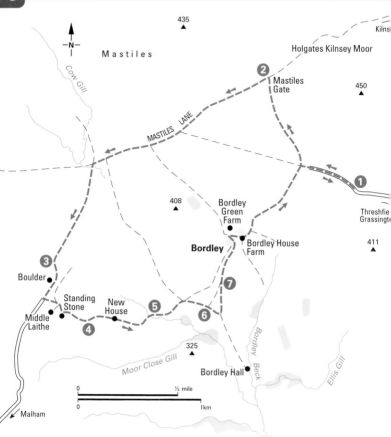

WALK 25 DIRECTIONS

1 From the parking place go through the gate and follow the metalled lane downhill to a crossroad of tracks. Turn right here, on to the track signposted 'Kilnsey'. Follow the track parallel with the dry-stone wall on your right to reach a crossing track at another signpost. This is Mastiles Gate.

2 Turn left along the lane signed 'Street Gate'. Follow the lane for 1 mile (1.6km), first climbing gently and then descending between walls into a shallow valley. Go through a gate and continue for about 100yds (91m) to a gate on the left from which a rough track heads down to ford a stream. Follow the rough track across the stream, over a slight rise and across rough pasture.

❸ Eventually it runs between walls, bearing right near a large triangular boulder. Continue down to meet a metalled lane and turn left to Middle Laithe. Walk through the farmyard and over a cattle grid. Follow the farm track, crossing a cattle grid by a National Trust sign for New House farm.

❹ Continue into a walled lane which leads into the farmyard of New House. Bear right through a gate then bear left down the field to a gate in the bottom left-hand corner. Go through the gate, turn left and follow the line of telegraph poles. Go over a stile and descend across the stream.

WHILE YOU'RE THERE

Visit Kilnsey Crag by the Wharfe where a great limestone cliff dominates the valley, with an overhanging nose that provides a severe test to climbers. The crag was formed when an ice age glacier ground away the end of a limestone spur as it made its way south from Littondale. Once, a lake lapped the crag's foot – it silted up long ago, leaving rich farm land.

❺ Climb away from the stream and bear right, then contour around the hillside. The path meets and follows a wall on your right. Go through the first gate on your right and follow the wall on your left, bearing right to go through a gap in the crossing wall.

❻ Turn left to go round the angle of the wall on your left to a stone stile in the crossing wall. Follow the wall on the left up the field, past a tumbled wall, to join a track.

❼ Turn right along the track and continue to a gate just above Bordley. Drop down right, then double back left to pass to the

WHERE TO EAT AND DRINK

Draw a circle of 4 miles (6.4km) in diameter centred on Bordley – and you will not find a pub or café. So before or after the walk head for Grassington, which has plenty of tea shops as well as several recommended pubs including the Foresters Arms, or try the Old Hall Inn at Threshfield.

right of the first stone barn to double gates. Beyond the gates turn right and follow the track past the farmhouse. Climb the metalled lane, which reverts to rough track as it levels out. Descend to the crossroads and turn right to ascend the hill back to the start.

WHAT TO LOOK OUT FOR

The merlin, Britain's smallest falcon, may sometimes be spotted above the moorland. The male has a blue-grey tail and back, while the larger female is brown-backed and has a banded tail. They most often nest on the ground, but have been known to occupy abandoned crows' nests. Like most falcons, their diet consists mainly of small mammals and insects, but more especially other birds, particularly ring ouzels and meadow pipits, which they catch in their swooping and spiralling flight.

Three Nidderdale Villages

*From Lofthouse to Ramsgill and Middlesmoor
in the valley of the River Nidd.*

DISTANCE 7 miles (11.3km) **MINIMUM TIME** 3hrs

ASCENT/GRADIENT 656ft (200m) ▲▲▲ **LEVEL OF DIFFICULTY** ✦✦✦

PATHS Mostly field paths and tracks; may be muddy, 18 stiles

LANDSCAPE Rich farmland and moorland, wide views from Middlesmoor

SUGGESTED MAP OS Explorer OL30 Yorkshire Dales – Northern & Central

START/FINISH Grid reference: SE 101734

DOG FRIENDLINESS Can be off lead on walled section between Studfold Farm
and Stean, but should be on lead for rest of walk

PARKING Car park by Memorial Hall in Lofthouse

PUBLIC TOILETS None en route

Much of upper Nidderdale was proposed as an Area of Outstanding Natural Beauty in 1947 – but official designation happened only in 1994. There were discussions as to whether the area should be included as part of the Yorkshire Dales National Park but Nidderdale was designated separately. It is an area of moorland wildness and deep, farmed valleys. In the late 19th and 20th centuries, parts of the dale were dammed as a chain of reservoirs – Angram, Scar House and Gouthwaite – was constructed to supply water to the city of Bradford.

Monks, Fairies and a Murderer

Throughout Nidderdale are small, stone-built settlements like those visited on the walk – many of them of considerable antiquity. The monks of Fountains Abbey, near Ripon, founded the attractive village of Lofthouse as a grange in the Middles Ages. It was one of the bases from which they controlled their vast farming interests in Nidderdale. Lofthouse today consists mainly of 19th-century cottages. Ramsgill, at the southern end of the route, is at the head of Gouthwaite Reservoir, which was opened in 1899 and is renowned for its spectacular bird life. The village was the birthplace, in 1704, of Eugene Aram, scholar and murderer, who arranged for the slaughter of his wife's lover and was hanged in Knaresborough for the crime – a deed retold by both Bulwer Lytton and the poet Thomas Hood. The village was also used in the feature film *Fairy Tale: A True Story* (1997) about two Yorkshire girls who hoaxed many – including Arthur Conan Doyle and Harry Houdini – into believing they had photographed fairies in Cottingley, near Bradford. In the third village, Middlesmoor, with its spectacular hilltop setting, the head of an Anglo-Saxon cross with its inscription to St Cedd in the church again indicates the age of a settlement which today seems to date mainly from the last two centuries.

It was once possible to travel from Pateley Bridge up the dale on Britain's only corporation-run light railway. The Nidd Valley Light Railway, originally laid as a narrow-gauge line by the builders of Angram Reservoir, was taken over by Bradford Corporation in 1907 and re-laid as standard gauge. It ran regular passenger services from Pateley Bridge (where it connected with the North Eastern Railway's line) to Lofthouse, with stations at Wath and what was called Ramsgill (but was really at Bouthwaite). It closed to passengers in 1929, but the track is still visible on much of the route.

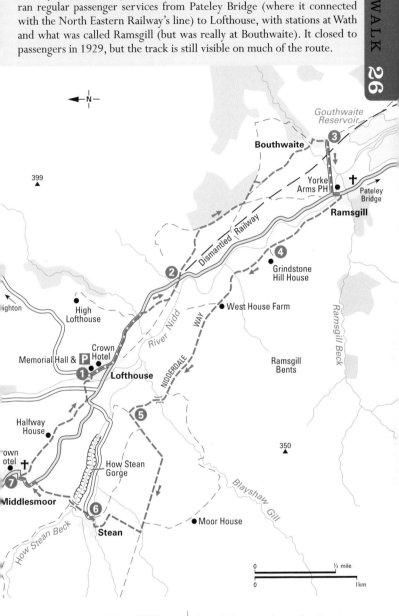

WALK 26 DIRECTIONS

❶ Walk downhill past the Crown Hotel. At the main road turn left. Just beyond the track to High Lofthouse farm go right, through a stile. Follow a clear track bending left to a waymarked stile, then bear left to another stile. Continue down to a slightly raised track (the old railway) and bear left to rejoin the road.

❷ Cross the road and go through a gate, signed Bouthwaite. Bear left off the farm track to a stile

WALK 26

and ascend a grassy ramp. Bear left to climb more steeply, then right towards a plantation. Follow a clear path just below the plantation. Pass a house then join a track and follow it past a gate and Nidderdale Way sign to a fork. Bear left, still parallel to the plantation, then turn right over a stile. Descend left of a farmhouse, then bear left to a tall ladder stile. Walk straight ahead, keep a wall to your right and descend into a wooded valley. Ignore a stile on the right and go through a waymarked gate, over a wooden bridge, through a metal gate and ahead. Bear right past a house down a gravelled track to a lane.

WHILE YOU'RE THERE

The attractive town of Pateley Bridge has many fascinating small shops, as well as walks by the River Nidd and the interesting Nidderdale Museum in King Street, housed in a former workhouse.

---

❸ Turn right down the lane to a T-junction. Turn left, over the bridge. Turn right by the triangular green, then right again, signed 'Stean'. Follow the track until it bends left up to Grindstone Hill House.

❹ Go straight on, over four stiles. At West House Farm go over a stile between the farm and a bungalow, cross the farm road, follow waymarked posts (Nidderdale Way) and continue along a track, eventually descending to a signpost near a

---

WHERE TO EAT AND DRINK

For top-of-the-range meals, the Yorke Arms in Ramsgill has an enviable reputation. There are also two Crown Hotels on or near the route, one in Lofthouse and another in Middlesmoor.

WHAT TO LOOK OUT FOR

The species of oil beetle, *meloë proscarabaeus,* have been sighted at Middlesmoor. Unlike other beetles, oil beetles' wing cases do not overlap, making them look as if they are wearing waistcoats. They also have kinked antennae – the male beetle's end with blobs. Oil beetles get their name from an oily fluid they secrete from their leg joints if they're disturbed. It deters predators and can cause blistering on human skin.

---

barn. Follow the obvious track into a valley and over a bridge.

❺ At a T-junction of tracks, turn left. Follow the walled track uphill, bending right. As the main track bends left to Moor House, keep straight on along a grassy track. Another track joins from the left. Just beyond this, after crossing a stream, turn right. Bend left by a farm and follow the track over a ford into Stean.

❻ Follow the lane right, then take a stile on the left signed 'Middlesmoor'. Descend into How Stean Gorge, down steps, over a bridge and up steps, then follow signs to the road. Turn left into Middlesmoor. Turn right beside the Wesleyan chapel to the gateway of the parish church.

❼ Turn right before the gate, through a stile signed 'Lofthouse'. Follow the path to Halfway House farm. Go through the farmyard to a gate and follow the right side of two fields then bear left across the third to a gate in the corner. In the lay-by go left through a gate, then along the path beside the cricket ground. Cross the lane and go over a bridge, then bear right to emerge near the Market Cross in Lofthouse. Turn left to the car park.

The Mines of Greenhow and Bewerley Moor

*Through a landscape of lead mining,
from one of Yorkshire's highest villages.*

DISTANCE *6 miles (9.7km)*   MINIMUM TIME *2hrs 45min*

ASCENT/GRADIENT *1,181ft (360m)* ▲▲▲   LEVEL OF DIFFICULTY ✦✦✦

PATHS *Field and moorland paths and tracks, 4 stiles*

LANDSCAPE *Moorland and valley, remains of lead mining industry*

SUGGESTED MAP *OS Explorer 298 Nidderdale*

START/FINISH *Grid reference: SE 128643*

DOG FRIENDLINESS *Dogs can be off lead for much of route*

PARKING *Car park at Toft Gate Lime Kiln*

PUBLIC TOILETS *None en route*

It is a long haul from Pateley Bridge up Greenhow Hill to the village of Greenhow, one of the highest in Yorkshire, at around 1,300ft (396m) above sea level. Until the early 17th century this was all bleak and barren moorland. When lead mining on a significant scale developed in the area in the 1600s, a settlement was established here, though most of the surviving buildings are late 18th and 19th century. Many of the cottages also have a small piece of attached farmland, for the miners were also farmers, neither occupation alone giving them a stable income or livelihood. In a way typical of such mining villages, the church and the pub – the Miners Arms, of course – are at the very centre.

Romans and Monks

Romans are the first known miners of Greenhow, though there is said to be some evidence of even earlier activity, as far back as the Bronze Age. The Romans had a camp near Pateley Bridge, and ingots of lead – called 'pigs' – have been found near by, dating from the 1st century AD. In the Middle Ages lead from Yorkshire became important for roofing castles and cathedrals – it is said that it was even used in Jerusalem. Production was governed by the major landowners, the monasteries, and some, like Fountains and Byland, became rich from selling charters for mining and from royalties. After the monasteries were dissolved, the new landowners wanted to exploit their mineral rights, and encouraged many small-scale enterprises in return for a share of the profits.

As you leave Greenhow and begin to descend into the valley of the Gill Beck, you pass through the remains of the Cockhill Mine. It is still possible to make out the dressing floor, where the lead ore was separated from the waste rock and other minerals, and the location of the smelt works, where the ore was processed. Beyond, by the Ashfold Side Beck, were the Merryfield Mines and, where the route crosses the beck, there are extensive remains of the Prosperous Smelt Mill. All these mines were active in the middle of the 19th century, and some had a brief resurgence in the middle of the 20th.

GREENHOW

Besides the Lead

The vast retaining banks of Coldstones Quarry rise above the car park at Toft Gate Lime Kiln. This enormous hole (you can see it from the viewing point at the top of the bank) opened in about 1900 and produces almost 1 million tons of limestone a year. Around Greenhow, the limestone layers are particularly deep, allowing large blocks to be cut. Across it run two mineral veins, called Garnet Vein and Sun Vein, both of which have been mined for lead and for fluorite. Other minerals found in smaller quantities in the rock here are barite, calcite and galena, as well as crystals of cerrusite, anglesite and occasionally quartz.

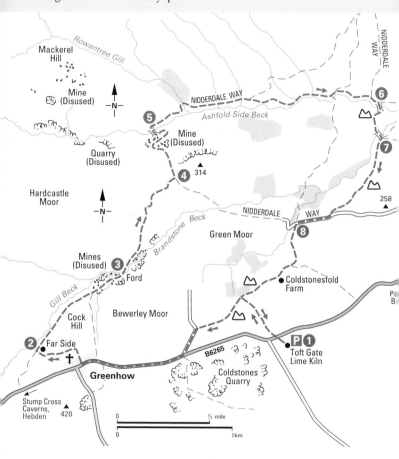

WALK 27 DIRECTIONS

❶ Cross the road from the car park and go over the stile opposite into a field. Follow the faint path downhill to a gate. Descend bearing left, passing above a barn. Cross another stile and descend to a metalled track. Turn left and walk up the hill to a road.

Turn left and walk up to the main road. Turn right and follow this down into Greenhow village. At the bottom of the hill, just past a converted chapel, take a lane to the right. At the junction go left and follow the lane to a cattle grid. Follow waymarks along the wire fence, round to the right to pass behind the house (Far Side).

GREENHOW

2 Follow the track past Low Far Side and down into the valley of Gill Beck and then Brandstone Beck, where there are the extensive remains of lead mining activity. Where the track swings left, keep straight on down through the scars and spoil heaps to meet another track at a ford.

3 Cross and follow the obvious track up the hill. Go over a stile beside a gate by trees then, 100yds (91m) beyond, take another stile on the right. Follow the track towards a house but before reaching it turn left between stone walls and descend to another stile and T-junction with another track.

4 Turn left and go through a waymarked gateway. Descend to spoil heaps then follow steep paths downhill just to the right of the heaps. Turn left by an iron cogwheel to a footbridge over Ashfold Side Beck.

5 Follow the path slanting up to the right to meet a track. Follow this down the valley, eventually going through a series of caravan sites. About 1 mile (1.6km) from the footbridge, the Nidderdale Way leaves the track at a signpost. Go straight on for another 100yds (91m), then turn right through a metal gate near a toilet block then over a bridge.

6 Climb the steep track away from the river and as the gradient eases go left on a green track between stone walls. Nearing a house, go right a few paces then cross a footbridge.

WHERE TO EAT AND DRINK

Sadly, the Miners Arms in Greenhow has closed, so either head west to Stump Cross Caverns and its tea room or east to Pateley Bridge, which is well served with hotels, pubs, restaurants and tea rooms. Apothecary's House serves light lunches and teas. Grassfields Country House Hotel in Low Wath Road has both a restaurant and a bistro in an elegant Georgian mansion.

7 Turn right through a gate and follow the rough track uphill. Meet another track at a T-junction and turn left, but as the track begins to bend left, bear right across the grass to a kissing gate and a metalled lane. Turn right.

8 About 100yds (91m) after passing Low Waite Farm on the right, fork left on a track. Just before a cattle grid, turn right and follow the rougher track up to Coldstonesfold Farm. Continue along the metalled track to a waymarked post on a bend, where you turn left to retrace your outward route and return to Toft Gate Lime Kiln.

WHAT TO LOOK OUT FOR

The lime kiln at Toft Gate is very well preserved and is now protected by English Heritage. It was built in the 1860s to help meet the Victorians' huge demand for lime, both in agriculture and building. The flue, chimney and main furnace are visible and you can also see inside the kiln itself, where interpretive panels explain the workings of the kiln.

A Medieval Walk from Fountains

*From the magnificent ruins of Fountains Abbey
to the fascinating medieval manor of Markenfield Hall.*

DISTANCE 6.5 miles (10.4km)	MINIMUM TIME *3hrs*
ASCENT/GRADIENT *328ft (100m)* ▲▲▲	LEVEL OF DIFFICULTY +++

PATHS *Field paths and tracks, a little road walking, 3 stiles*

LANDSCAPE *Farmland and woodland*

SUGGESTED MAP *OS Explorer 298 Nidderdale*

START/FINISH *Grid reference: SE 270681*

DOG FRIENDLINESS *Dogs should be on leads on field paths*

PARKING *Car park at west end of Abbey, or at visitor centre*

PUBLIC TOILETS *Fountains Abbey visitor centre*

After you have climbed the hill from the car park and begun the walk along the valley side, following the ancient abbey wall, the south front of Fountains Hall is below you. Built by Sir Stephen Proctor in 1611, it is a fine Jacobean House, with lots of mullioned windows and cross gables. Were it anywhere other than at the entrance to Fountains Abbey, it would be seen as one of the great houses of the age. Sir Stephen was, by all accounts, not the most scrupulous of men, having made his huge fortune as Collector of Fines on Penal Statutes. Nor did he respect the Abbey buildings; the stone he built his house with was taken from the south-east corner of the monastic remains.

Abbey and Abbot

A little further along the path, the Abbey ruins come into view. When monks from St Mary's Abbey in York first settled here in 1132, it was a wild and desolate place. Nevertheless their abbey prospered, and became one of the country's richest and most powerful Cistercian monasteries. More remains of Fountains than of any other abbey ruin in the country. Its church was 360ft (110m) long. The other buildings, laid out along (and over) the River Skell, give a vivid impression of what life was like here in the Middle Ages. All came to an end in 1539 when King Henry VIII dissolved the larger monasteries. This was only a few years after Abbot Marmaduke Huby had built the huge tower, a symbol of what he believed was the enduring power of his abbey.

Mr Aislabie's Garden

Beyond Fountains Abbey are the pleasure gardens laid out between 1716 and 1781 by John Aislabie and his son William. John had retired to his estate here at Studley Royal after being involved – as Chancellor of the Exchequer – in the financial scandal of the South Sea Bubble. It is one of the great gardens of Europe, contrasting green lawn with stretches of water, both formal and informal. Carefully placed in the landscape are ornamental buildings, from classical temples to Gothic towers. The

FOUNTAINS ABBEY

Aislabie's mansion stood at the north end of the park; it was destroyed by fire in 1945.

The highlight of the southern end of the walk is Markenfield Hall, a rare early 14th-century fortified manor house, built around 1310 for the Markenfield family. You can see the tomb of Sir Thomas Markenfield and his wife Dionisia in Ripon Cathedral. Open for four weeks in the summer, the house still clearly demonstrates how a medieval knight and his family lived; it is part home, part farm. You can see the chapel and the great hall. The gatehouse, convincingly medieval, is 200 years younger than the house.

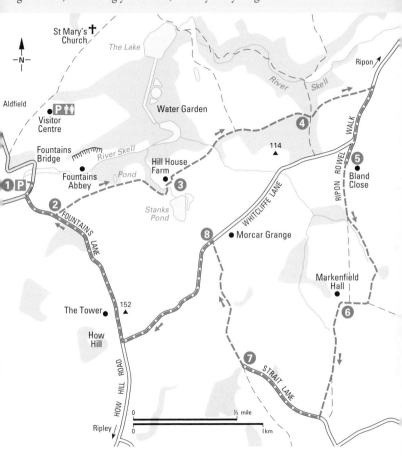

WALK 28 DIRECTIONS

❶ From the car park turn right uphill, signed 'Harrogate'. At the fork go left, signed 'Markington, Harrogate'. Just after the road bends right, go left at a footpath sign through a gate.

❷ Follow the grassy path just inside the ancient Abbey wall,

past a small pond. Go through a waymarked gate and follow the track as it curves round to the right through another gate, then bend left to a gate into Hill House Farm.

❸ Turn right then follow the footpath signs to go left at the end of a large shed and then right. Go through a metal gate on to a track. At the end of the hedge, go ahead

FOUNTAINS ABBEY

down the field to a gate into the wood. Follow the track, passing the ruined archway, to descend to a crossroads.

❹ Go straight on, signed 'Ripon'. The track climbs to a gate with a Ripon Rowel Walk sign. Follow the track beside the line of trees to a gate on to Whitcliffe Lane. Turn right. At the top of the rise go straight ahead on the metalled road.

❺ Go over the cattle grid by Bland Close, then leave the lane to go straight ahead with the hedge on your right to a gateway. Continue along the waymarked track, eventually with woodland to your right. Follow the park wall through a gateway to reach a gate on to a lane. Turn right to reach some farm buildings by Markenfield Hall.

❻ Follow the wall to the left, going through a metal gate and straight ahead down the track, over a stile by a gate. Follow the track, then a waymark sign, across a field

to a stile by a gate. Turn right up the narrow Strait Lane, to emerge into a field.

❼ Follow the waymarked path beside the hedge. Go through a gate in the field corner and continue ahead with the hedge to the right. Go through two more gates. At a third gate, do not go through, but bend left through a hedge gap and down the field side, with the hedge on your right, to go through a gate on to Whitcliffe Lane.

❽ Turn left and follow the lane, which leads in the direction of How Hill Tower, an 18th-century folly, to a T-junction. Turn right and follow the road back to the car park.

Along the Canal at Gargrave

*Following the Leeds and Liverpool
Canal from Gargrave.*

DISTANCE *3.5 miles (5.7km)*   MINIMUM TIME *1hr 30min*

ASCENT/GRADIENT *114ft (35m)* ▲▲▲   LEVEL OF DIFFICULTY ✚✚✚

PATHS *Field paths and tracks, then canal tow path, 1 stile*

LANDSCAPE *Farmland and canal bank*

SUGGESTED MAP *OS Explorer OL2 Yorkshire Dales – Southern & Western*

START/FINISH *Grid reference: SD 931539*

DOG FRIENDLINESS *Dogs should be on leads, except on the canal bank*

PARKING *Car park near village hall, signed from A65*

PUBLIC TOILETS *By bridge in Gargrave*

Gargrave has long been a stopping-off point for travellers from the cities of West Yorkshire on their way to the coast at Morecambe or to the Lake District. These days, most of them arrive along the A65 from Skipton, the route formerly taken by horse-drawn coaches. There is still evidence of the village's importance as a coaching centre, especially at the Old Swan Inn. Its position beside the River Aire had also proved important when 18th- and 19th-century surveyors were seeking westward routes for other methods of transport; the walk crosses the railway not long after leaving Gargrave (this is the route that, not far west, becomes the famous Settle-to-Carlisle line) and you will return to the village beside the Leeds and Liverpool Canal.

Earlier Settlers, Mills and Bandages

Although Gargrave is today mostly a 19th-century settlement, there is evidence that the area has been in occupation much longer. The site of a Roman villa has been identified nearby, while on West Street excavation has found the remains of a moated homestead dating from the 13th century, with a smithy and a lime pit, that was reused in the 15th century. By the 18th century, there were cotton mills in Gargrave, served by the canal, and weavers were engaged in producing cloth for the clothing industry. Their expertise resulted in the establishment here of one of the village's biggest employers, Johnson & Johnson Medical, where they found workers who could undertake the fine weaving that was needed to produce their bandages.

Canal Digging

In October 1774 the eastern arm of the Leeds and Liverpool canal, snaking its way westwards from Leeds, reached Gargrave. The route, surveyed by John Longbotham and approved by the great canal-builder James Brindley, had been agreed in 1770. Work began at both the Liverpool and the Leeds ends, but there were, inevitably, arguments between the separate committees in Yorkshire and Lancashire about both the route and the finances.

GARGRAVE

It was not until 1810 that the canal had crossed the Pennines, and barges could go from Leeds to Blackburn, and only in 1816 was the full distance of 127 miles (204km) open to Liverpool. Gargrave benefited not only from the access it gave the village to the raw materials for the cotton mills and the chance to export its cloth, but also as a stopping-place for the bargees.

The walk joins the canal near the lowest of the six locks at Bank Newton, where the canal begins a serpentine course to gain height as it starts its trans-Pennine journey. Near the lock is the former canal company boatyard where boats for maintaining the canal were built. As you walk along the tow path, you will cross the Priest Holme Aqueduct, where the canal passes over the River Aire.

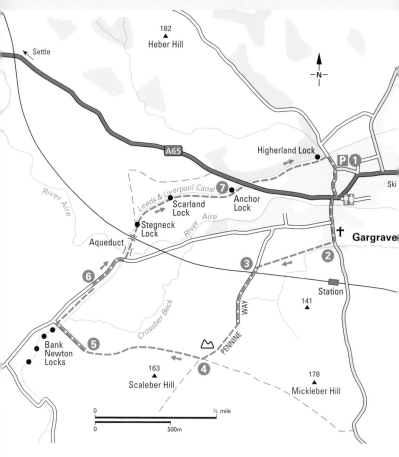

WALK 29 DIRECTIONS

❶ Walk down the lane, past Gargrave Village Hall. At the main road turn right, cross the road and go left into Church Street and over the bridge. Pass the church on your left. Just past Church Close House on your right, turn right, following

a Pennine Way sign. Go over a stone stile in the wall on your left.

❷ Turn right along the wall, following the Pennine Way path, which is partly paved here. Go ahead across the field to a waymarked gate, then half left to another gate. Walk up the field, left of power lines, to a gate that leads to a rough sunken lane.

❸ Turn left, over a railway bridge, then follow the track up a small hill. Cross a cattle grid, then leave the track to cross a stile on the left into a field. Take a faint path half-right then join a track, making for a signpost on the skyline.

❹ At the post, turn right to the corner of a wire fence, then slant down a grassy ramp to reach a waymarked gate in a crossing fence. Go ahead across the field to a pair of gates. Take the waymarked left-hand one and continue ahead, at first following a fence and line of trees. Continue straight ahead to meet a track and turn right.

❺ Follow the track down to the canal by Bank Newton Locks. Cross the bridge and turn right along the tow path. Where the tow

path runs out, join the lane which runs alongside the canal.

❻ Go ahead along the lane, cross the bridge over the canal then turn right down a spiral path to go under the bridge and continue along the tow path. Pass over a small aqueduct over the river, then under a railway bridge. Continue past Stegneck Lock and Scarland Lock to reach Anchor Lock.

❼ Beyond the lock, opposite the Anchor Inn, go under the road bridge and continue along the tow path to reach Bridge 170, at Higherland Lock. Go on to the road by a signpost. Turn right down the road, back to the car park.

River and Woodland at Bolton Abbey

*Over moorland and alongside
the Strid to the romantic priory.*

DISTANCE 6.75 miles (10.9km)   MINIMUM TIME 2hrs 30min

ASCENT/GRADIENT 870ft (265m) ▲▲▲   LEVEL OF DIFFICULTY ✦✦✦

PATHS Field and moorland paths, then riverside tracks, 3 stiles

LANDSCAPE Moorland with wide views and riverside woodland

SUGGESTED MAP OS Explorer OL2 Yorkshire Dales – Southern & Western

START/FINISH Grid reference: SE 071539

DOG FRIENDLINESS Must be on lead in woodland and on moorland

PARKING Main pay-and-display car park at Bolton Abbey

PUBLIC TOILETS By car park and at Cavendish Pavilion

Bolton Abbey has always been one of the showpieces of the Yorkshire Dales, and attracts many visitors, most of whom stay close to the monastic buildings or venture only to the Strid. This walk takes you a little further afield, and has the priory – it was never an abbey – as its climax. After passing under the archway – in fact an aqueduct built in the 18th century to carry water to a mill – you reach Bolton Hall. In part originally the gateway to Bolton Priory, this was later extended as a hunting lodge for the Earls of Cumberland and their successors the Dukes of Devonshire, who still own the estate. The wings are said to be by Sir Joseph Paxton, designer of the Crystal Palace. The walk then passes westwards through woodland to the top of a hill offering excellent views west towards the Aire Valley and north over Barden Fell.

The Thundering Strid

At the entrance to the woodland around the Strid there are information boards that explain the birds and plants you can find here, including the sessile oak. Characteristic of the area, it is distinguished from the pedunculate oak by the fact that its acorns have no stalks. At the Strid itself the River Wharfe thunders through a narrow gorge between rocks. The underlying geology is gritstone, with large white quartz pebbles embedded in it. The Strid was a place loved by the Victorians, but the flow is fast and the river is 30ft (9m) deep here with strong eddy currents, so don't be tempted to cross; there have been many drownings here over the years. A little further on is the Cavendish Pavilion. A survivor from the early years of the 20th century, the pavilion, called after the family name of the Dukes of Devonshire, has been restored and added to over the years, and is still reminiscent of leisurely sunny days in the 1920s.

The priory was built for Augustinian canons who founded their house here in 1154. The ruins make one of the most romantic scenes in the country, and all the great English artists, from Girtin and Turner on, have painted it. Much of what remains was complete by 1220; the last prior, unaware of the coming storm that would sweep away monastic life, began

Opposite: Graveyard and ruins of Bolton Priory near Skipton (Walk 30)

BOLTON ABBEY

a tower at the west end. It remained unfinished when the monasteries were suppressed. Most of the buildings fell into ruin, but the nave of the priory church was given to the local people, and it is still their parish church. A former rector, William Carr, spent 54 years here, laying out the paths along the valley that are now enjoyed by so many visitors.

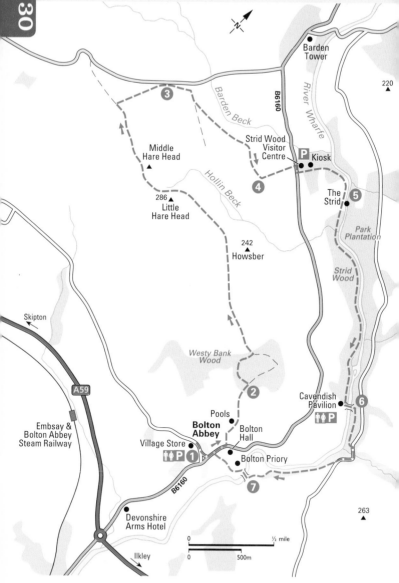

WALK 30 DIRECTIONS

1 Leave the car park at its north end, by the Village Store. Turn right and walk to the B6160.

Turn left and follow the road under an archway. Opposite the battlemented Bolton Hall, turn left on a signed track. At the top of the track, go through a gate on the right with a bridleway sign. Walk under a power line to a signpost. Go past two pools to a gate, then bear right to another gate into woodland.

② Follow the rising track through the wood, with several signs, to another gate. Follow blue waymarks, most painted on rocks, across fields. At a crest bear left to a gate in a corner, then turn left along the wall. The path climbs more steeply onto Hare Head, which has wide views. Descend gently to a gate, and 20yds (18m) beyond, take a path downhill, trending right lower down, to a signpost.

WHERE TO EAT AND DRINK

Bolton Abbey is well-supplied with refreshment places. The Cavendish Pavilion has snacks, light meals and afternoon teas. The Priest's House at Barden Tower, about 1 mile (1.6km) north of the entrance to Strid Wood, has a restaurant and tea terrace. The Devonshire Arms Country House Hotel, with its Brasserie and Burlington restaurant liess south of the start.

③ Turn right on a path, parallel to the road, to another signpost 'FP to B6160'. Follow the track to a stile, then take the left fork, going roughly level across the moor, to a wall corner. Continue to the next wall, then turn right along it, following an improving track to a signpost.

WHILE YOU'RE THERE

Take a trip on the Embsay and Bolton Abbey Steam Railway, which has a station 1.5 miles (2.4km) south of the Priory. Operated by enthusiasts, the railway runs steam trains at weekends, and on most days in August; at other times there is a historic diesel service.

④ Turn left over a stile and follow the wall down to the road. Turn right a few paces then enter the car park. Pass beside the Strid Wood Visitor Centre and follow tracks, signed 'The Strid', down to reach the river close to its narrowest part at the Strid.

⑤ Follow wide tracks downstream until you reach an information board and gateway near the Cavendish Pavilion. Bear left by the café and cross the footbridge.

⑥ Immediately after the bridge turn right, signed 'Bolton Abbey'. The path briefly joins a vehicle track to cross a side-stream then bears right. When the path forks, take either branch (the higher has better views of the priory). Descend to a bridge beside stepping-stones near the priory.

⑦ Cross the bridge and walk straight on. Climb steps to a gateway – the Hole in the Wall. Go through to the road, left a few paces, then right to the car park.

WHAT TO LOOK OUT FOR

Bolton Priory church is a mix of Norman and later styles – look out for the tell-tale round Norman arches and the pointed arches of the later work. The west front is very complicated – it has a huge, decorative window, but masks an even better 13th-century west front. The eastern end of the church is in ruins but look out for the memorable remains of the huge east window. The nave, now the parish church, still gives an impression of the building's original grandeur. The stained-glass windows, on the right-hand side as you enter, date from the first half of the 19th century and were designed, in convincing medieval style, by Augustus Pugin, whose decorative work is found in the Houses of Parliament.

Gisburn Forest – a Walk in the Woods

Wooded valleys and heathland – accompanied by the sounds of woodland birds and waterfowl.

DISTANCE **3 miles (4.8km)**   MINIMUM TIME **1hr 30min**

ASCENT/GRADIENT **285ft (87m)** ▲▲▲   LEVEL OF DIFFICULTY **+++**

PATHS **Forest tracks and footpaths**

LANDSCAPE **Wooded valleys, forest, beckside heathland**

SUGGESTED MAP **OS Explorer OL41 Forest of Bowland & Ribblesdale**

START/FINISH **Grid reference: SD 732565**

DOG FRIENDLINESS **Fine for dogs under reasonable control**

PARKING **Stocks Reservoir car park, Gisburn Forest (free of charge)**

PUBLIC TOILETS **None en route**

Perfectly placed between the Yorkshire Dales and the Forest of Bowland, Gisburn Forest in the Upper Hodder Valley is the setting for this short, circular stroll. Don't be put off because it's in a forest – it certainly isn't a dire trek through the darkness of a dense conifer plantation. You will walk along open, naturally wooded valleys, beside a tumbling beck and over heathland. You will have views over the reservoir and up to the fells, and you will hear the woodland birdsong and the call of the wildfowl on the water. If you're lucky, you may spot a deer, footprints in the sandy earth confirm their presence.

Stocks Reservoir

The two defining aspects of this walk are the open waters of Stocks Reservoir and the woodlands of Gisburn Forest. The reservoir was built in the 1930s to provide drinking water for the towns of central Lancashire. The village of Stocks was submerged in the process along with many ancient farmsteads. The date stone from one of these can now be seen over the doorway of the post office in Tosside. It was formed by damming the River Hodder and can hold 2.6 billion gallons (12 billion litres) of water when it is at full capacity.

Attractively placed on the edge of the forest, the reservoir is now an important site for wildfowl and 30 different species visit during the average winter period. Amongst the less-commonly sighted of these are red-throated divers, whooper swans, gadwalls and great crested grebes. Amongst the different birds of prey who frequent the area, ospreys and peregrine falcons have been spotted, as well as a rare passing marsh harrier. A birdwatching hide is provided for budding ornithologists, and a pleasant permissive footpath has been constructed around the shoreline.

The Forestry Commission's extensive woodland known as Gisburn Forest was developed at the same time as the reservoir and was opened by HRH Prince George in July 1932. It covers 3,000 acres (1,214ha), making it the largest single forested area in Lancashire. There are several waymarked trails to be enjoyed, and a cycle network has been developed

GISBURN FOREST

which extends to over 10 miles (16.1km). Although the majority of the plantations are of the monotonous coniferous variety and are managed principally as a commercial crop, more and more broadleaf trees are being planted to improve the visual aspect and to increase the diversity of wildlife. The forest and the reservoir are now managed in tandem, with inputs from United Utilities, the Forestry Commission and local parishes, to develop a sustainable economic base for this beautiful landscape.

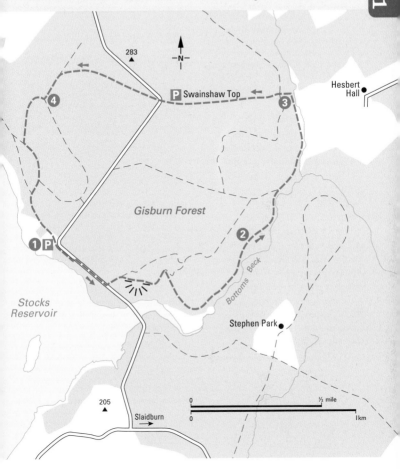

WALK 31 DIRECTIONS

❶ Leave Stocks Reservoir car park at the right of the two vehicular entrances. Follow a path right of the road until it bends away; cross the road then continue on the other side, still parallel to the road, until you reach a broad forest track. Turn left; a red marker post soon confirms your route. There are good views right,

through the trees to the reservoir and causeway with the fells in the background. Keep on the track as it takes you beside open wooded valleys and through natural woodland with a river down on your right.

❷ Pass a short track down to the right. Soon the main track forks; take the narrower right branch, through a sort of cutting, then

WHERE TO EAT AND DRINK

Nothing is available within the forest itself, so it might be an idea to pack a picnic. Alternatively, head 4.5 miles (7.2km) south-west to Slaidburn, where you'll find the popular Riverbank Café (closed Mondays in winter). Just up the village street is the famous 13th-century Hark to Bounty Inn, which serves good bar meals. If you're heading east, the Dog and Partridge at Tosside has good ale and a diverse menu.

bear right and down towards the river. The track soon divides but the two branches rejoin further on. The right branch runs close to the tumbling peaty Bottoms Beck, with fields rising to Hesbert Hall beyond it.

3 After the two branches of the paths merge again, two red marker posts in quick succession direct you up and left on a rougher path. Meet a forest track, go a few paces right then left again on a continuation path. Follow it gently uphill and almost dead straight, passing upright gateposts by a collapsed ruin. Walk through

Swinshaw Top car park to the road and go straight over to take a narrow footpath through the woods by another red marker post. The path opens on to a broadish green swathe but is soon closed in again; however, lovely elevated views over the reservoir, left, and the fells ahead make the start of your descent pleasurable.

WHILE YOU'RE THERE

The Forest of Bowland is a designated Area of Outstanding Natural Beauty (AONB) occupying the north-eastern corner of Lancashire. It is a landscape of barren gritstone fells, moorland and steep-sided valleys, with 3,260 acres (1,320ha) of open country available to walkers. The village of Dunsop Bridge in the Trough of Bowland claims to be the official centre of the country – a telephone box adjacent to the village green marks the precise spot.

4 Meet a forest track at a bend, proceed straight ahead (slightly right) and follow the track for 200yds (183m) until red posts turn you right, down a footpath with a stream on the right. At a T-junction of footpaths, turn left across open heathland on a clear path back to the car park.

WHAT TO LOOK OUT FOR

It's more a case of what to listen for! The birdsong throughout the walk, from tiny wrens darting into the bushes in front, to the cry of the curlew skyward is symphonic. Add to that the call of the wildfowl on the reservoir, never far away, and the orchestration is complete.

LOTHERSDALE

Tucked Away in Secluded Lothersdale

A short walk with fine views and a glimpse of Lothersdale's industrial past.

DISTANCE 4 miles (6.4km)   MINIMUM TIME 2hrs

ASCENT/GRADIENT 1,509ft (460m) ▲▲▲   LEVEL OF DIFFICULTY +++

PATHS Tracks and field paths, some steep sections. 8 stiles

LANDSCAPE Pennine moorland, farmland and industrial relics

SUGGESTED MAP OS Explorer OL21 South Pennines

START/FINISH Grid reference: SD 939472

DOG FRIENDLINESS Off lead on final section of walk, from Point ❺ onwards

PARKING Roadside parking on Carleton to Colne road, north of Clogger Lane

PUBLIC TOILETS None en route

WALK 32

Set deep in the rolling countryside to the west of Keighley, Lothersdale is a village of gritstone houses and mill buildings – typical of the small settlements that grew up in the late 18th and early 19th centuries along the river valleys of the West Riding of Yorkshire. The mill dam that you will cross as you enter the village is characteristic of the scale of the industrial enterprise undertaken then – sufficient to employ local people, but too small to fight against the expanding trade of its larger neighbours. Farming and industry had always co-existed here, and today Lothersdale relies on agriculture and tourism – it is a popular stop on the Pennine Way – as well as its role as a base for those who work in the West Yorkshire conurbation.

In the Quarry

The Lothersdale district is of particular interest to geologists. As part of the Ribblesdale Fold Belt, there is a notable anticline at Lothersdale, where the limestone has been tilted by the forces of the earth so that it dips significantly – at angles of anything from 20 to 90 degrees from the horizontal. This dramatic effect is best studied at Raygill Quarry, to the west of the village, where the crest of the anticline is exposed in the rock faces. Between 1876 and 1895 over 35,000 tons of barytes was mined at Raygill. This valuable mineral is a sulphate of barium, which is used in drilling processes, as well as in industrial coatings and linings. The quarrying of the fine carboniferous limestone here continued well into the 20th century, but has now ceased, and the flooded quarry workings have been transformed into a successful trout fishery. Raygill was also the site of a discovery, in 1880, of the bones and teeth of several mammals that died in fissures in the rocks in the period between the ice ages. They included remains of mammoth, rhinoceros, lions, bear, bison and hyena. The bones were taken to Leeds City Museum, where they were damaged by bombing during the Second World War.

Friends and Scholars

The Society of Friends has had a long association with Lothersdale. This once-remote valley provided a haven for Quakers in the persecutions of

LOTHERSDALE

the 17th century. They built a meeting house here in 1723 and enlarged it in 1799. It had a gallery with unusually designed hatches that could close to create a separate room. The meeting house closed in 1959. In 1800 the Lothersdale Quakers opened one of the earliest Sunday schools anywhere in the world, 'for the preservation of the youth of both sexes, and for their instruction in useful learning.'

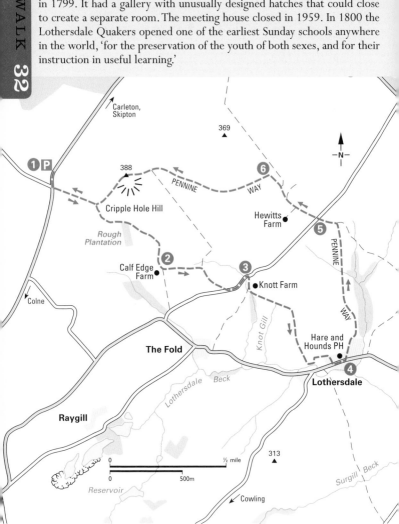

WALK 32 DIRECTIONS

❶ From the car park walk downhill towards the mast on the next hilltop. Just before the cattle grid, turn left up a signed track. At the next signpost turn right, off the track. Follow the wall, then bear left to cut off the corner as it bends left. Soon cross a stile in the wall on your right. Bear left, above a small plantation, then go diagonally right. Go over a stile and continue downhill with a wall on your right, which bends left to reach a signed stile on to a metalled drive.

❷ Turn left along the drive. After the cattle grid, bear right along a concrete road and over another cattle grid. Emerge on to a metalled lane and turn left. Follow the lane as it dips to cross a small stream, then immediately turn right.

LOTHERSDALE

3 Follow the track, which bends left below a house, then continues across a field with a wall on your left. From the next gate bear right to another gate and continue down, following the wall on the left towards a pool in the valley. Cross a stile in the corner, turn left immediately through a gate and in a few paces go left and up to join a track. Turn right and follow it to the road. Turn left. Just beyond the Hare and Hounds pub, turn left at the Pennine Way sign.

4 Follow the track uphill to a Pennine Way sign. Turn left here to follow the fence and then the wall on your left, crossing a small stream. Continue straight ahead to a stile beside a gate on your left, signed with an acorn. Go straight across the field to a stone stile on to a lane.

5 Cross the lane and continue up the track ahead, signed 'Pennine Way'. Where the concrete farm track bends left, go straight ahead over a stone stile on to a walled track. Where the walls open out, follow the one on your left to a stile, then continue to follow the wall on your left to where it bends sharply left.

6 Follow the wall left, go over two plank bridges and continue along the well-worn path, past occasional cairns to the trig point on the hilltop. Follow either of the two downhill paths, which soon rejoin, and continue past the signpost you passed near the start of the walk. Continue downhill to the road and turn right to return to the car parking place.

Along the Wharfe to a Victorian Spa Town

*From Addingham to Ilkley, along a stretch
of the lovely River Wharfe.*

DISTANCE 5.5 miles (8.8km)	**MINIMUM TIME** 2hrs 30min
ASCENT/GRADIENT 360ft (110m) ▲▲▲	**LEVEL OF DIFFICULTY** ✦✦✦
PATHS Riverside path and field paths, some road walking, 7 stiles	
LANDSCAPE Rolling country and the River Wharfe	
SUGGESTED MAP OS Explorer 297 Lower Wharfedale	
START/FINISH Grid reference: SE 083498	
DOG FRIENDLINESS Keep on lead on minor roads	
PARKING Lay-by at eastern end of Addingham, on bend where North Street becomes Bark Lane by information panel	
PUBLIC TOILETS Ilkley	

Addingham is not one of those compact Yorkshire villages that huddles around a village green. The houses extend for 1 mile (1.6km) on either side of the main street, with St Peter's Church at the eastern end of the village, close to the river. So it's no surprise that the village used to be known as 'Long Addingham', and that it is actually an amalgamation of three separate communities that grew as the textile trades expanded. Having been by-passed in recent years, Addingham is now a quiet backwater.

Within 50 years, from the end of the 17th century, Addingham's population quadrupled, from 500 to 2,000. Even here, at the gateway to the Yorkshire Dales, the textile industries flourished. At the height of the boom, there were six woollen mills in the village. Low Mill, built in 1787, was the scene of a riot by a band of Luddites – weavers and shearers who objected to their jobs being done by machines. Though the mill itself was demolished in 1972, more houses were added to the mill-hands' cottages to create Low Mill Village, a pleasant riverside community.

Ilkley

Visitors from, say, Bath or Cheltenham should feel quite at home in Ilkley, a town that seems to have more in common with Harrogate, its even posher neighbour to the north-east, than with the textile towns of West Yorkshire. The Romans established an important fort here – believed to be 'Olicana' – on a site close to where the parish church is today. Two Roman altars were incorporated into the base of the church tower, and in the churchyard can be found three Anglo-Saxon crosses that date back to the 9th century. One of the few tangible remains of the Roman settlement is a short stretch of wall near the handsome Manor House, which is now a museum.

Like nearby Harrogate, Ilkley's fortunes changed dramatically with the discovery of medicinal springs. During the reign of Queen Victoria, the great and the good would come here to 'take the waters' and socialise at the town's hydros and hotels. Visitor numbers increased with the coming of the railway, and included such luminaries as Madame Tussaud, George Bernard

ADDINGHAM

Shaw and Charles Darwin, taking a well-earned rest after the publication of *On the Origin of Species*.

With its open-air swimming pool and riverside promenades, Ilkley was almost an inland resort. Though we have replaced water cures with more sophisticated quackery, Ilkley remains a prosperous town, unashamedly dedicated to the good things of life.

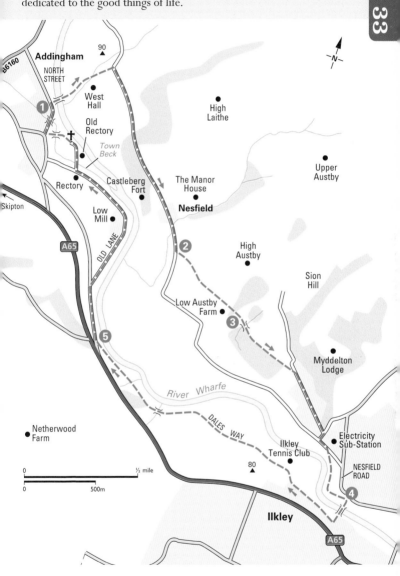

WALK 33 DIRECTIONS

❶ Walk 50yds (46m) up the road, and take stone steps down to the right, (signed 'Dales Way'). Bear immediately right again, and cross

the River Wharfe on a suspension bridge. Follow a metalled path along a field edge. Turn over a stream at the end and follow a farm track left to emerge on the bend of a minor road. Go right here;

after about 0.5 mile (800m) of road walking you reach the little community of Nesfield.

2 About 100yds (91m) beyond the last house, and immediately after the road crosses a stream, bear left up a stony track (signed as a footpath to High Austby). Immediately take a stile between two gates. Cross to the gate in the far-right corner. Through it, there is no obvious path, but follow the boundary on your right, heading towards Low Austby Farm. Approaching the buildings, waymarks indicate the path dog-legging left and right outside the boundary wall, passing beneath a gnarled oak towards a wood.

> ### WHERE TO EAT AND DRINK
> In Addingham try The Sailor or The Fleece for traditional pub food. At the bottom end of Ilkley you are close to 'The Taps' or the Ilkley Moor Vaults as it officially called, and the Riverside Hotel, which is particularly child-friendly.

3 Cross a footbridge over a stream; beyond a stile you enter woodland. Follow a path downhill, leaving the wood by another step stile. Bear right across the slope of a field to a stile at the far end, to enter more woodland. Follow an obvious path through the trees, before reaching a road via a wall stile. Go right, downhill, to reach a road junction. Go right again, crossing Nesfield Road, and take a path to the left of an electricity sub-station. You have a few minutes of riverside walking before you reach Ilkley's old stone bridge.

4 Cross the bridge. This is your opportunity to explore the spa town of Ilkley. Otherwise you should turn right, immediately after the bridge, on to a riverside

path (from here back to Addingham you are following the well-signed Dales Way). At its end, keep ahead along a drive to Ilkley Tennis Club. Beside the clubhouse, bear off left through a kissing gate and follow an obvious path across a succession of pastures, which eventually returns you to the River Wharfe. Cross a stream on a footbridge, and enter woodland. Cross another stream to meet a stony path. Go right, downhill back to the river. Through another kissing gate, walk the length of a riverside meadow before joining the old A65 road. Thanks to the by-pass it is now almost empty of traffic.

5 Follow the road right by the riverside. After almost 0.5 mile (800m) of road walking, go right, just before a row of terraced houses, on to Old Lane. Carry on between the houses clustered at its end – Low Mill Village – to locate a riverside path at the far side. Once you have passed the Rectory on the left, and the grounds of the Old Rectory on your right, look for a gate on the right. Take steps and follow the path to a tiny arched bridge over Town Beck. Swing left across a pasture, in front of the church. Cross a drive to another arched bridge, walking out between old stone cottages onto North Street in Addingham.

> ### WHILE YOU'RE THERE
> Addingham lies at the north-western edge of the county. Just 1 mile (1.6km) to the north you enter the Yorkshire Dales National Park. By following the B6160 you soon come to Bolton Abbey, with its priory ruins in an idyllic setting by a bend in the River Wharf (see Walk 30).

Ilkley Moor and the Twelve Apostles

Standing stones and a brief look at some of the intriguing historic features which make up Ilkley Moor.

DISTANCE 4.5 miles (7.2km)   MINIMUM TIME 2hrs 30min

ASCENT/GRADIENT 803ft (245m) ▲▲▲   LEVEL OF DIFFICULTY +++

PATHS Good moorland paths, some steep paths towards end of walk, no stiles

LANDSCAPE Mostly open heather moorland and gritstone crags

SUGGESTED MAP OS Explorer 297 Lower Wharfedale

START/FINISH Grid reference: SE 132467

DOG FRIENDLINESS Under control where sheep graze freely on moorland

PARKING Car park below Cow and Calf rocks

PUBLIC TOILETS Public toilets at White Wells

Ilkley Moor is a long ridge of millstone grit, immediately to the south of Ilkley. With or without a hat, Ilkley Moor is a special place… not just for walkers, but for lovers of archaeological relics too. These extensive heather moors are identified on maps as Rombalds Moor, named after a legendary giant who roamed the area. But, thanks to the famous song – Yorkshire's unofficial anthem – Ilkley Moor is how it's always known.

An Ancient Ring

The Twelve Apostles is a ring of Bronze Age standing stones sited close to the meeting of two ancient routes across the moor. If you expect to find something of Stonehenge proportions, you will be disappointed. The twelve slabs of millstone grit (there were more stones originally, probably twenty, with one at the centre) are arranged in a circle approximately 50ft (15m) in diameter. The tallest of the stones is little more than 3ft (1m). The circle is, nevertheless, a genuinely ancient monument.

The Twelve Apostles are merely the most visible evidence of 7,000 years of occupation of these moors. There are other, smaller circles too, and Ilkley Moor is celebrated for its Bronze Age rock carvings, many showing the familiar 'cup and ring' designs. The most famous of these rocks features a sinuous swastika: traditionally a symbol of good luck, until the Nazis corrupted it. There are milestones, dating from more recent times, which would have given comfort and guidance to travellers across these lonely moors. In addition to Pancake and Haystack rocks, seen on this walk, there are dozens of other natural gritstone rock formations. The biggest and best known are the Cow and Calf, close to the start of this walk, where climbers practise their holds and rope work.

A guidebook of 1829 described Ilkley as a little village. It was the discovery of mineral springs that transformed Ilkley into a prosperous spa town. Dr William Mcleod arrived here in 1847, recognised the town's potential and spent the next 25 years creating a place where well-heeled hypochondriacs could 'take the waters' in upmarket surroundings.

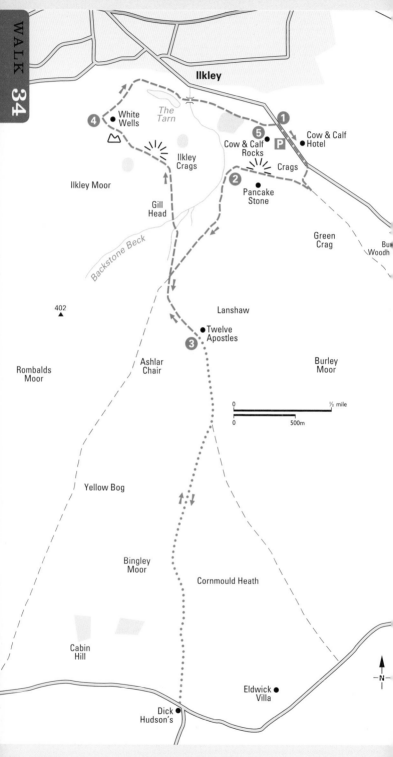

Ilkley

White
Wells

4

The
Tarn

Ilkley
Crags

1

Cow & Calf
Rocks

5

P

Cow & Calf
Hotel

Crags

2

Pancake
Stone

Ilkley Moor

Gill
Head

Green
Crag

Bu
Woodh

Backstone Beck

402

Lanshaw

Twelve
Apostles

3

Rombalds
Moor

Ashlar
Chair

Burley
Moor

0   ½ mile

0   500m

Yellow Bog

Bingley
Moor

Cornmould Heath

Cabin
Hill

—N—

Eldwick
Villa

Dick
Hudson's

ILKLEY MOOR

Dr Mcleod recognised – or perhaps imagined – the curative properties of cold water. He vigorously promoted what he called the 'Ilkley Cure', a regime of exercise and cold baths. Luxurious hotels known as 'hydros', precursors of today's health farms, sprang up around the town to cater for visitors.

Predating the town's popularity as a spa is White Wells, built in 1700 around one of the original springs. A century later a pair of plunge baths were added, where visitors and locals alike could enjoy the masochistic pleasures of bathing in cold water. Enjoying extensive views over the town, the building is still painted white. White Wells is now a visitor centre that's open to visitors at weekends and bank holidays.

WALK 34 DIRECTIONS

❶ Walk up the road; 150yds (137m) beyond the Cow and Calf Hotel, where the road bears left, fork right up a grassy path. Scramble on to the ridge and follow it west past the Pancake Stone, enjoying extensive views over Ilkley and Wharfedale. Dip across a path rising along a shallow gully and continue beyond Haystack Rock, joining another path from the left. Keep left at successive forks, swinging parallel to the broad fold containing Backstone Beck, over to the right

❷ Gently rise for 0.75 mile (1.2km) across open moor, until the path meets the Bradford–Ilkley Dales Way link. Go left here, along a section of duckboarding. Pass a boundary stone at the top of the rise, and continue to the ring of stones known as the Twelve Apostles, just beyond the crest.

❸ Retrace your steps from the Twelve Apostles, but now continue ahead along the Dales

WHILE YOU'RE THERE
Ilkley Moor is criss-crossed by old tracks. You could explore for weeks without walking the same path twice. An east–west walk from the Cow and Calf will take you along the moorland ridge, with terrific views of Ilkley and Wharfedale for most of the way.

WHAT TO LOOK OUT FOR
Many rocks on Ilkley Moor are decorated with 'cup and ring' patterns – including the Pancake Stone, near the start of this walk. Many more rock carvings can be found if you take the time to search for them.

Way link. Bear right at a fork and cross the head of Backstone Beck. Shortly, beyond a crossing path, the way curves left in a steep, slanting descent off the moor below the ridge, levelling lower down as it bends to White Wells.

❹ Turn right in front of the bathhouse and follow a path across the slope of the hill past a small pond and below a clump of rocks to meet a metalled path. Go right, taking either branch around The Tarn to find a path leaving up steps at the end. After crossing Blackstone Beck, ignore a rising grass track and continue up the final pull to the crags by the Cow and Calf rocks.

❺ It's worth taking a few minutes to investigate the rocks and watch climbers practising their belays and traverses. From here a paved path leads back to the car park.

EXTENDING THE WALK
A classic extension of this walk takes you across the moor from the Twelve Apostles (Point ❸) to the pub at Dick Hudson's, returning by the same route.

In Giant Rombald's Footsteps

A taste of West Yorkshire moorland from the village of Burley in Wharfedale.

DISTANCE	4.5 miles (7.2km) MINIMUM TIME 2hrs
ASCENT/GRADIENT	754ft (230m) ▲▲▲ LEVEL OF DIFFICULTY +++
PATHS	Good tracks and moorland paths, 3 stiles
LANDSCAPE	Moor and arable land
SUGGESTED MAP	OS Explorer 297 Lower Wharfedale
START/FINISH	Grid reference: SE 163458
DOG FRIENDLINESS	Can be off lead but watch for grazing sheep
PARKING	Burley in Wharfedale Station car park
PUBLIC TOILETS	At railway station

According to the legend, a giant by the name of Rombald used to live in these parts. While striding across the moor that now bears his name (in some versions of the story he was being chased by his angry wife) he dislodged a stone from a gritstone outcrop, and thus created the Calf, of the Cow and Calf rocks. Giants such as Rombald and Wade – and even the Devil himself – were apparently busy all over Yorkshire, dropping stones or creating big holes in the ground. It was perhaps an appealing way of accounting for some of the more unusual features of the landscape.

Rombalds Moor is pitted with old quarries, from which good quality stone was won. The Cow and Calf rocks used to be a complete family unit, but the rock known as the Bull was broken up to provide building stone.

The Hermit of Rombalds Moor

At Burley Woodhead a public house called The Hermit commemorates Job Senior, a local character with a chequered career. Job worked as a farm labourer, before succumbing to the demon drink. He met an elderly widow of independent means, who lived in a cottage at Coldstream Beck, on the edge of Rombalds Moor. Thinking he might get his hands on her money and home, Job married the old crone. Though she died soon after, Job took no profit. The family of her first husband pulled the cottage down, in Job's absence, leaving him homeless and penniless once more.

Enraged, he built himself a tiny hovel from the ruins of the house. Here he lived in filth and squalor on a diet of home-grown potatoes, which he roasted on a peat fire. He cut a strange figure, with a coat of multi-coloured patches and trousers held up with twine. He had long, lank hair, a matted beard and his legs were bandaged with straw. He made slow, rheumatic progress around Rombalds Moor with the aid of two crooked sticks.

His eccentric lifestyle soon had people flocking to see him. He offered weather predictions, and even advised visitors about their love lives. The possessor of a remarkable voice, he 'sang for his supper' as he lay on his bed of dried bracken and heather. These impromptu performances encouraged Job to sing in nearby villages, and even in the theatres of Leeds and Bradford.

His speciality was sacred songs, which he would deliver with great feeling. Nevertheless, his unwashed appearance meant that accommodation was never forthcoming, forcing him to bed down in barns or outhouses.

It was while staying in a barn that he was struck down with cholera. He was taken to Carlton Workhouse, where he died in 1857, aged 77. A huge crowd of people gathered at his funeral. Job Senior, the hermit of Rombalds Moor, was buried in the churchyard of Burley in Wharfedale. He's commemorated in the old sign hanging over the entrance at The Hermit.

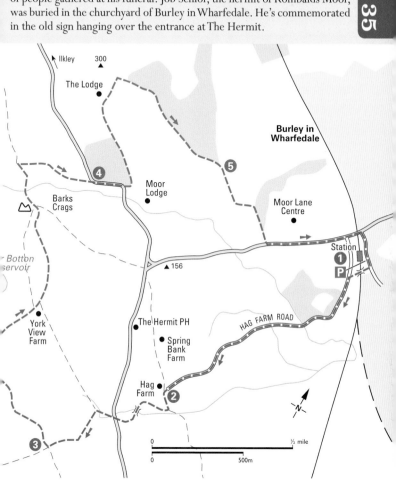

WALK 35 DIRECTIONS

1 From the station car park, cross the line via a footbridge and go left along a quiet lane. Follow the lane past houses and between fields up to Hag Farm.

2 When the track wheels right, into the farmyard, keep left on a track to a stile and a gate. Accompany a wall downhill for 100yds (91m) to a gap stile in the wall. Don't pass through, but instead turn right, climbing beside a stream up to a stile. Carry on uphill, crossing another stile and then a footbridge spanning the stream. Continue up to cottages, winding out between them to meet the Guiseley–Ilkley road. (To visit The Hermit you would need to go right here for 0.25 mile/400m.) Cross the road and

BURLEY IN WHARFEDALE

Rombalds Moor is home to the red grouse, often claimed to be the only truly indigenous British bird. They take off from their heather hiding places with heart-stopping suddenness, with their cry of 'go back, go back, go back'. Their moorland habitat is carefully managed to maintain a supply of young heather for the grouse to nest and feed in. This concern with their welfare has a commercial imperative. Grouse shooting is lucrative and the season begins on the 'Glorious Twelfth' of August.

continue on a stony track opposite. Keep ahead where it splits and then swing left to ford a stream. Follow a path uphill through trees and then between walls to a gate. Turn right beside the wall, which soon curves away, leaving you heading upwards on a trod.

❸ Meet a stony track and follow it to the right, along the moorland edge. Follow a wall to a stile by a gate. Immediately after, keep right when the track forks. Keep right again as you approach a small brick building. Route-finding is now easy, as the track wheels around a farm. Branch off left at the next farm (called York View because on a clear day, you can see York Minster from here) to make a slow descent, following a wall on your right. As you approach a third farm, look out for two barns and a gate, on the right. They stand opposite an indistinct path

to the left, which curves around a small quarry. Enjoy level walking through bracken with great views over Lower Wharfedale. After 0.25 mile (400m), drop into a narrow ravine to cross Coldstone Beck. As you climb away, bear right and follow a path downhill to meet a road by a sharp bend.

WHERE TO EAT AND DRINK

The Hermit in Burley Woodhead is a welcoming stone-built pub with oak-panelled and beamed rooms. Its name recalls an eccentric local character. Alternatively, the village of Burley in Wharfedale also boasts a number of places to get a bite to eat.

❹ Walk 100yds (91m) down the road, to another sharp bend. Turn off along Stead Lane, a stony track which leads past a couple of houses to continue between the fields beyond. After passing a wooden chalet, leave the track as it swings left towards a farm, dropping through a kissing gate to the right. Walk away beside the wood on your left. Beyond another kissing gate, keep by the right-hand boundary, leaving at the far side to follow a walled path ahead.

❺ Reaching a track, go right, but after 200yds (183m), bear off left along a path which leads to a second track within trees. Follow it right to the road and go left back to the station.

WHILE YOU'RE THERE

Harry Ramsden's in nearby Guiseley is not just a fish-and-chip restaurant, but also a Yorkshire institution. The Harry Ramsden chain now stretches from the Epcot Centre in Florida to Inverness in Scotland, but this is the real thing, the original. It was founded here, in a little hut, in 1928 by the eponymous Harry Ramsden. A Bradford-based fish frier of some repute, Harry had been forced to sell up and move to the country by his wife's tuberculosis. The location, at the terminus of tram routes from both Bradford and Leeds, proved to be a profitable one.

Golden Acre and Breary Marsh

*A walk of great variety in the rolling
countryside to the north of Leeds.*

DISTANCE 5.5 miles (8.8km)   MINIMUM TIME 2hrs 30min

ASCENT/GRADIENT 246ft (75m) ▲▲▲   LEVEL OF DIFFICULTY +++

PATHS *Good paths, tracks and quiet roads, 20 stiles*

LANDSCAPE *Parkland, woods and arable country*

SUGGESTED MAP *OS Explorer 297 Lower Wharfedale*

START/FINISH *Grid reference: SE 266417*

DOG FRIENDLINESS *On lead when in park, due to wildfowl*

PARKING *Golden Acre Park car park, across road from park itself, on A660 just south of Bramhope*

PUBLIC TOILETS *Golden Acre Park, at start of walk*

Leeds is fortunate to have so many green spaces. Some, like Roundhay Park, are long established; others, like the Kirkstall Valley nature reserve, have been created from post-industrial wasteland. But none have had a more chequered history than Golden Acre Park, 6 miles (9.7km) north of the city on the main A660.

Amusement Park

The park originally opened in 1932 as an amusement park. The attractions included a miniature railway, nearly 2 miles (3.2km) in length, complete with dining car. The lake was the centre of much activity, with motor launches, dinghies for hire and races by the Yorkshire Hydroplane Racing Squadron. An open-air lido known, somewhat exotically, as the Blue Lagoon, offered unheated swimming and the prospect of goose-pimples. The Winter Gardens Dance Hall boasted that it had 'the largest dance floor in Yorkshire'.

Though visitors initially flocked to Golden Acre Park, the novelty soon wore off. By the end of the 1938 season the amusement park had closed down and was sold to Leeds City Council. The site was subsequently transformed into botanical gardens – a process that's continued ever since. The hillside overlooking the lake has been lovingly planted with trees and unusual plants, including rock gardens and fine displays of rhododendrons.

The boats are long gone; the lake is now a haven for wildfowl. Within these 127 acres (51ha) – the 'Golden Acre' name was as fanciful as 'the Blue Lagoon' – is a wide variety of wildlife habitats, from open heathland to an old quarry. Lovers of birds, trees and flowers will find plenty to interest them at every season of the year. One of the few echoes of the original Golden Acre Park is a café situated close to the entrance.

Reflecting the park's increasing popularity with local people, a large car park has been built on the opposite side of the main road, with pedestrian access to the park via a tunnel beneath the road. This intriguing park offers excellent walking, both pushchairs and wheelchair have access to the circuit of the lake on a broad path.

GOLDEN ACRE PARK

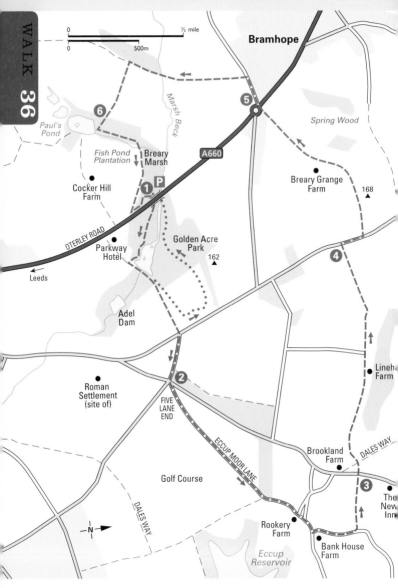

WALK 36 DIRECTIONS

1 From the southern corner of the car park, take steps and an underpass beneath the road, into Golden Acre Park. Take either of the paths to the left or the right around the lake to its far end, leaving the park by a gate (signed 'Meanwood Valley Trail'). Bear left, along a tree-lined path, to a

T-junction of roads. Take the road ahead, up to the aptly-named Five Lane End.

2 Take the second road on the left (Eccup Moor Road), shortly passing a golf course on the right. Ignore side turnings till you reach the outbuildings of Bank House Farm, where you take a waymarked bridleway to the left. It soon narrows to become a path between hedgerows. About 50yds (46m) before the footpath bears right, take a stile in the fence on your left, to join a field path to a wall stile. Cross another field to meet a road (The New Inn is just along the road to your right).

3 Go left along the road for just 20yds (18m) to take a stile on your right (signposted 'Dales Way'). Keep ahead over an intersection to join another track, which leads to a gate and stile. Carry on for 150yds (137m) by the boundary to a waypost and bear right across the pasture to a stile in the end wall. Walk on towards Lineham Farm, bypassing it through a couple of kissing gates to meet a track. Go right and immediately left to pick up an enclosed grass track. When it finishes, maintain your direction beside successive fields to reach a road.

WHAT TO LOOK OUT FOR

Look for the damp-loving alder trees in Breary Marsh. Their seeds are designed to float on the water. During winter you should see little siskins (a type of finch) feeding on the seeds, of which they are particularly fond. You may also spy the vivid caterpillar of the alder moth.

4 Go right for 150yds (137m) and take a waymarked kissing gate on the left. Follow the field-edge path with a fence on your left. Through two more kissing gates, bear left across a field, keeping to the right of Breary Grange Farm. After a ladder stile, keep ahead to another stile at the far corner. Head left, across the next field, to a stile that brings you out at the A660 by a roundabout.

WHERE TO EAT AND DRINK

It requires the shortest of detours, at about the half-way point of this walk, to visit The New Inn, near Eccup. A sign welcomes walkers – as do the open fires and beer garden – and an extensive menu will whet your appetite. Within Golden Acre Park, you'll find the Bakery Coffee House, offering everything from a snack to a full meal.

5 Cross the main road and take The Sycamores ahead. After 250yds (229m), take a waymarked kissing gate on the left to join a field-edge footpath with a hedge on the left. Cross a succession of three stiles and the tiny Marsh Beck, before skirting an area of woodland on your right. Over a final stile, go left on a track to a farmhouse, continuing beyond over a stile on a field path to a gate into Fish Pond Plantation.

6 Bear right through the wood, soon reaching the banked dam of a small pool, Paul's Pond. There is a pleasant path around its bank, but the way back lies to the left, along a woodland path accompanying a stream. Over a footbridge lower down, continue through the trees. Reaching a junction, go left along a duck-boarded walkway across Breary Marsh to the underpass by the car park.

WHILE YOU'RE THERE

Take a look at Bramhope's Puritan Chapel, adjacent to the entrance to the Britannia Hotel, on the A660 as it passes through the village. This small, simple chapel was built in 1649 by devout Puritan Robert Dyneley. Although generally locked, peering through the windows reveals its original furnishings, including box-pews and a three-deck pulpit.

Harewood's Treasure House

A stately home with parkland by 'Capability' Brown, a few miles from Leeds.

DISTANCE 7 miles (11.3km)   MINIMUM TIME 3hrs

ASCENT/GRADIENT 672ft (205m) ▲▲▲   LEVEL OF DIFFICULTY ✦✦✦

PATHS Good paths and parkland tracks all the way, 2 stiles

LANDSCAPE Arable and parkland

SUGGESTED MAP OS Explorer 289 Leeds or 297 Lower Wharfedale

START/FINISH Grid reference: SE 334450

DOG FRIENDLINESS Keep under control through estate and on A659

PARKING Limited in Harewood village. From traffic lights, take A659, and park in first lay-by on left

PUBLIC TOILETS None en route; in Harewood House if you pay to go in

The grand old houses of West Yorkshire tend to be in the form of 'Halifax' houses. Self-made yeomen and merchant clothiers built their mansions, to show the world that they'd made their 'brass'. But Harewood House, on the edge of Leeds, is more ambitious, and is still one of the great treasure houses of England.

Vision into Reality

The Harewood Estate passed through a number of wealthy hands during the 16th and 17th centuries, eventually being bought by the Lascelles family who still own the house today. Edwin Lascelles left the 12th-century castle in its ruinous state, to overlook the broad valley of the River Wharfe, but demolished the old hall. He wanted to create something very special in its place and hired the best architects and designers to turn his vision into reality.

John Carr of York created a veritable palace of a house, in an imposing neo-classical style and laid out the estate village of Harewood too. The interior of the building was designed by Robert Adam, now best remembered for his fireplaces. Thomas Chippendale, born in nearby Otley, made furniture for every room, as part of the house's original plans. The foundations were laid in 1759; 12 years later the house was finished. Inside the house are paintings by JMW Turner and Thomas Girtin, who both stayed and painted at the house. Turner was particularly taken with the area, producing pictures of many local landmarks. The sumptuous interior, full of family portraits, ornate plasterwork and silk hangings, is in sharp contrast to life below stairs, in the kitchen and scullery.

The house sits in extensive grounds, which were preened and groomed to be every bit as magnificent as the house. They were shaped by Lancelot 'Capability' Brown, the most renowned designer of the English landscape. In addition to the formal gardens, he created the lake and the woodland paths you will take on this walk. Like so many of England's stateliest homes, Harewood House has had to earn its keep in recent years. The bird garden was the first commercial venture, but now the house hosts events such as

HAREWOOD

art exhibitions, vintage car rallies and even open-air concerts. This would make a good morning walk, with lunch at the Harewood Arms Hotel – perhaps followed by a tour of the house itself in the afternoon.

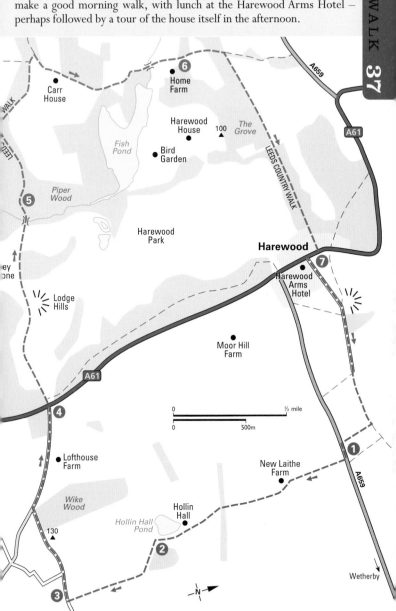

WALK 37 DIRECTIONS

1 From the lay-by walk 50yds (46m) away from the village of Harewood, cross the road and walk right, down the access track to New Laithe Farm. Keep to the left of the farm buildings, on a grassy track heading into the valley bottom. Go through two gates and bear half left up a field, towards Hollin Hall. Keep left of the buildings to pass Hollin Hall Pond.

2 Beyond the pond take a gate and follow a track to the left, uphill, skirting woodland. Continue uphill on a field-edge path with a hedgerow to your left. Pass through two gates, the path now being enclosed between hedges.

WHILE YOU'RE THERE

The walk takes you through the grounds of Harewood House but you need to pay if you want to investigate the house itself, the bird gardens, or the many other attractions.

3 Go right at the top of the hill to have easy, level walking on an enclosed sandy track (now following the Leeds Country Way). Keep straight ahead past a junction, through a gate. Skirt woodland to emerge at a road; go right here to arrive at the main A61.

4 Cross the road to enter the Harewood Estate (via the right-hand gate, between imposing gateposts). Follow the broad track ahead, through landscaped parkland, soon getting views of Harewood House to the right. Enter woodland through a gate, turning immediately left after a stone bridge.

5 Bear right at a fork after 100yds (91m) and keep with the main track. Later, at a crossing of tracks, go right, dropping to another junction. Turn right again but then fork left, leaving the trees to pass a farm, Carr House. Approaching the lake, the way swings left over a cattle grid before rising beside a high wall to a metalled drive. Bear left past a house and keep straight ahead at crossroads. Cross a bridge and follow the lane up to a gate, soon passing Home Farm (now converted to business units).

WHERE TO EAT AND DRINK

Apart from designing the house itself, John Carr was also responsible for the estate village of Harewood. The neat terraced houses have architectural echoes of the big house. Almost opposite the main gates of Harewood House is the Harewood Arms Hotel, a former coaching inn that offers the chance of a drink or meal towards the end of the walk. If the weather is kind, you can rest your legs in the beer garden.

6 Follow the road through pastureland, keeping right, uphill, at a choice of routes. Continue through woodland until you come to the few houses that comprise the estate village of Harewood.

7 Cross the main A61 road and walk right, for just 50yds (46m), to take a metalled drive immediately before the Harewood Arms Hotel. Beyond Maltkiln House, the way continues as a gated field track, opening great views over Lower Wharfedale. Carry on through a second gate for a further 350yds (320m) to a junction and go right over a cattle grid along a permissive bridleway, regaining the A659 beside the lay-by.

WHAT TO LOOK OUT FOR

The red kite used to be a familiar sight but numbers had dwindled to just a few pairs, mostly in Wales, due to centuries of persecution. There is now a new initiative to reintroduce the red kite to Yorkshire, and a number of birds have been released at Harewood House. You may be lucky enough to spot one.

Wetherby and the River Wharfe

*Around a handsome country market town
and along a stretch of the mature River Wharfe.*

DISTANCE 4 miles (6.4km)   **MINIMUM TIME** 2hrs

ASCENT/GRADIENT 164ft (50m) ▲▲▲   **LEVEL OF DIFFICULTY** ✦✦✦

PATHS Field paths and good tracks, a little road walking, no stiles

LANDSCAPE Arable land, mostly on the flat

SUGGESTED MAP OS Outdoor Leisure 289 Leeds

START/FINISH Grid reference: SE 404480

DOG FRIENDLINESS No particular problems

PARKING Free car parking in Wilderness car park, close to river, just over bridge
as you drive into Wetherby from the south

PUBLIC TOILETS Wetherby

Wetherby, at the north-east corner of the county, is not your typical West Yorkshire town. Most of the houses are built of pale stone, topped with roofs of red tiles – a type of architecture more usually found in North Yorkshire. With its riverside developments and air of prosperity, the Wetherby of today is a favoured place to live. The flat, arable landscape, too, is very different to Pennine Yorkshire. Here, on the fringes of the Vale of York, the soil is rich and dark and productive – the fields divided up by fences and hedgerows rather than dry-stone walls.

Historic Town

The town has a long history. A brief glance at an Ordnance Survey map reveals that Wetherby grew up around a tight curve in the River Wharfe. Its importance as a river crossing was recognised by the building of a castle, possibly in the 12th century, of which only the foundations remain. The first mention of a bridge was in 1233. A few years later, in 1240, the Knights Templar were granted a royal charter to hold a market in Wetherby.

At Flint Mill, passed on this walk, flints were ground for use in the pottery industry of Leeds. The town also had two corn mills, powered by water from the River Wharfe. The distinctive, restored weir helped to maintain a good head of water to turn the waterwheels. In general though, the Industrial Revolution made very little impression on Wetherby.

The town grew in importance not from what it made, but from where it was situated. In the days of coach travel, the 400-mile (644km) trip between London and Edinburgh was quite an ordeal for passengers and horses alike. And Wetherby, at the half-way point of the journey, became a convenient stop for mail and passenger coaches. The trade was busiest during the second half of the 18th century, when the town had upwards of 40 inns and alehouses. Coaching inns such as The Swan, The Talbot and The Angel catered for weary travellers and provided stabling for the horses. The Angel was known as 'the Halfway House' and had stables for more than a hundred horses. The Great North Road ran across the town's splendid

WETHERBY

WALK 38

arched bridge, and right through the middle of the town. With coaches arriving and departing daily, it must have presented a busy scene.

When the railway arrived in the 1840s, Wetherby's role as a staging post went into decline. The Great North Road was eventually re-routed around the town, and became known simply as the A1. More recently it has been upgraded to motorway status as the A1(M). When Dr Beeching wielded his axe in 1964, Wetherby lost its railway too. Ironically, a town that had once been synonymous with coach travel is now a peaceful backwater, re-inventing itself once again as an upmarket commuter town. The area around the River Wharfe has been renovated, to provide riverside apartments, pleasant walks and picnic sites. These days most people will probably know the town from listening to the racing results.

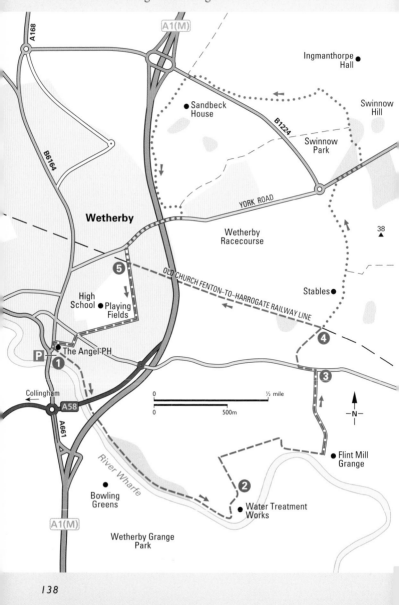

WALK 38 DIRECTIONS

1 Walk to the far end of the car park, to follow a path at the foot of low cliffs beside the River Wharfe. You pass in quick succession beneath the shallow arches of three modern bridges, carrying the A58 and A1(M) roads across the Wharfe. Emerging beyond, walk the length of a narrow pasture, passing through a kissing gate at the far end by Wetherby's water treatment works. Go left here, up a track around the perimeter fence.

2 After 150yds (137m) you meet a metalled track at the works' main entrance; go left here. At the top of an incline, where the track bears slightly to the right, there is a choice of routes. Your path is sharp right, along a grassy track between fields. You soon approach the wooded slope that overlooks the River Wharfe. Carry on beside the line of trees towards a farm, Flint Mill Grange.

3 Entering the farmyard, take the farm access road to the left. Meet Walton Road and walk left for 75yds (69m); then go right, along a metalled drive (this is signed as both a bridleway and the entrance to Wetherby Racecourse). After 0.25 mile (400m) you reach a gate, through which the longer walk continues along the drive ahead.

4 To return directly to Wetherby, however, turn left, dropping onto the trackbed of the old Church

Fenton-to-Harrogate railway line, which carried its last train in 1964. A mile's (1.6km) easy walking takes you to the A1(M) motorway, raised up on an embankment as it skirts around Wetherby. Take the underpass beneath the road, and keep ahead along Freemans Way, until you meet Hallfield Lane, (where extended walk rejoins).

5 Walk left, along Hallfield Lane, following it right around the playing fields of Wetherby High School towards the town centre. At the end, bear left into Nags Lane, right along Victoria Street and then go left back to the river.

EXTENDING THE WALK

You can extend the walk to see more of Wetherby's famous racecourse by leaving the main walk at Point **4** and following firstly a waymarked bridleway and then Sandbeck Lane, before crossing the motorway bridge to return to the main walk at Point **5**.

To Pendle with Witches and Water

Up Ogden's reservoirs to the inspiring viewpoint atop
Pendle Hill to discover witchcraft and folklore.

DISTANCE 4.5 miles (7.2km)	**MINIMUM TIME** 2hrs 30min
ASCENT/GRADIENT 1,095ft (334m) ▲▲▲	**LEVEL OF DIFFICULTY** +++

PATHS Defined paths, lots of kissing gates, one stile

LANDSCAPE Wooded valleys, moorland, hilltop views

SUGGESTED MAP OS Explorer OL41 Forest of Bowland & Ribblesdale

START/FINISH Grid reference: SD 823403

DOG FRIENDLINESS On lead near livestock on moorland

PARKING Pay-and-display car park in Barley

PUBLIC TOILETS At car park

This walk commences in the commendable village of Barley, which, in 1324, was known as Barelegh – an infertile lea or meadow. It follows much of the route of the Pendle Way, signposted by a black witch flying on her broomstick across a yellow sky. You climb gently past the Lower Ogden Reservoir and the Upper Ogden Reservoir to the steep sided Ogden Clough, then strike off up Boar Clough where the vegetation is indicative of acidic peat: ferns uncurl above bilberry shrubs and verdant patches of moss and white bog cotton complete the patchwork. The going is soft on the peaty ground across Barley Moor to the summit of Pendle Hill, and such is the spellbinding spirit of the area that dark figures on the skyline above could easily be mistaken for witches! The descent down the Big End is steep but quick, followed by a lovely tree-lined walk beside a tiny beck to return to Barley.

Referred to as a sleeping lion, Pendle Hill slopes gently up the lion's back to fall away sharply down the face, known as the Big End. The summit affords a spectacular birds-eye view over the Ribble Valley to Yorkshire's Three Peaks in the north and Lancashire's cotton towns of Padiham and Burnley nestling beneath the Pennine hills to the south. At 1,827ft (557m), the hill is constructed of gritstone and limestone, a combination that strongly influences the contrasting Pendle scenery. On the summit is the Beacon, a Bronze-Age burial mound thought to be possibly 7,000 years old. It was Pendle Hill that George Fox climbed in 1652 and where he had his vision of enlightenment that led him to found the Quaker movement. 'I was moved of the Lord to go up the top of it, which I did with much ado, as it was so very steep and high.'

Pendle Witches

Witch comes from the Anglo-Saxon word wicca, meaning 'the wise ones' who thought they possessed magical powers that could be put to use at times of pagan ritual. The Demdikes of Malkin Tower and the Chattox's of Higham were matriarchal families who terrorised the Pendle area in the early 17th century. These self-confessed witches were accused of cursing cattle and turning them into cats, turning the ale in the inn at Higham sour and bewitching the landlord's son to death, and paralysing a pedlar on the road to Colne. These were difficult times for independent women, witches or not and some 19 Pendle residents were eventually taken to the gaol at Lancaster Castle where they were charged with witchcraft. The Witch Trial took place in August 1612 and, after some dubious confessions, resulted in the execution by hanging of nine Pendle women.

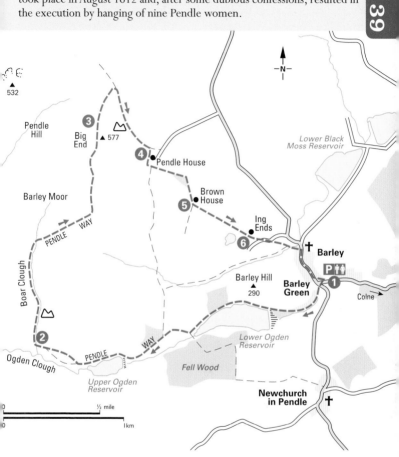

WALK 39 DIRECTIONS

❶ Exit the car park, turn right and cross the main road to a bridlepath signposted 'Ogden Clough', Pass the three-storey Barley Green Farmhouse with its interesting row of corbels, proceed between circular gateposts, and pass a Water Works building on the right. Continue to a climb beside the grassy dam of the lower reservoir, where the metalled lane gives way to an

unmade track. Continue straight ahead and join the Pendle Way as it leaves Fell Wood on the left; here you get your first clear view of Pendle Hill up to the right. Keep straight ahead to the bottom of the upper reservoir, cross a stile and ascend the track beside the dam. Follow the Pendle Way alongside the reservoir and up Ogden Clough, passing through a kissing gate into open country. The path is obvious to another kissing gate, where the route bears right up a stony path that soon swings left and follows the contours.

2 Cross the stream in Boar Clough. An obvious, badly eroded, path climbs up to the right. The worst of this can be avoided by continuing ahead a short distance, then climbing grassy slopes directly to a marker post. Either way is steep at first but soon gives way to a more gentle climb on soft ground along a cairn-marked route over Barley Moor to the summit trig point.

3 Walk along the summit escarpment to a wall with a ladder stile. Go right, staying this side of the wall, to a carved upright stone marking the Pendle Way; strike sharp right and descend steeply down the stone-stepped path.

WHAT TO LOOK FOR
Pendle's thick blanket of peat supports significant types of flora including sedges, cranberry, crowberry, and if you're lucky, you might spot some cloudberry (sometimes known as mountain strawberry). Bearing fruit in June and July, look for the little orange clusters of berries.

4 Go right after the kissing gate at the bottom, signposted 'Barley', rounding the back of Pendle House to a yellow-topped post and bear left through another gate. Drop down the meadow, with a wall on the left, and through a gate at the bottom leading into another meadow. Keep on down to a kissing gate and walk through

WHERE TO EAT AND DRINK
Barley has a selection of places for refreshments: the Tea Rooms offer home-made pies and broth with dumplings; the Barley Mow restaurant and the Pendle Inn each offer appropriate facilities.

WHILE YOU'RE THERE
Visit Wycoller Country Park, south-east of Colne, where the centrepiece is ruined Wycoller Hall, believed to be Ferndean Manor in Charlotte Brontë's Jane Eyre. It's a beautiful, atmospheric location – a remote upland valley which survived industrialisation and depopulation. There are waymarked walks, a picnic site, tea room and craft shop.

newly-planted trees to another gate near a farm building. Turn right along a track as signposted, then bear left through the grounds of Brown House to join a pretty tree-lined path between a stream and a wall.

5 Proceed through gates and over footbridges to reach a narrow cobbled lane. Exit onto a metalled road and turn left through the grounds of Ing Ends.

6 Soon cross a yellow waymarked footbridge on the right and bear left through a meadow and gates to pick up the stream on the left. On reaching the main road in Barley opposite the Primitive Methodist church, turn right through the village to a Pendle Way marker leading you off the road, through the playground and park to the car park beyond.

Laycock and Goose Eye

*A varied walk, from intimate woodlands
to the breezy moor-tops.*

DISTANCE 8 miles (12.9km)	**MINIMUM TIME** 4hrs

ASCENT/GRADIENT 1,230ft (375m) ▲▲▲   **LEVEL OF DIFFICULTY** +++

PATHS Good paths and tracks, take care with route finding, 8 stiles

LANDSCAPE Wooded valley and heather moorland

SUGGESTED MAP OS Explorer OL21 South Pennines

START/FINISH Grid reference: SE 032410

DOG FRIENDLINESS Under control where sheep graze on sections of moorland

PARKING In Laycock village, roadside parking at Keighley end of village, close to village hall

PUBLIC TOILETS None en route

To the west of Keighley a tranche of moorland sits astride the border between Yorkshire and Lancashire. Here you can walk for miles without seeing another hiker – and perhaps with just curlew and grouse for company. When we think of textile mills, we tend to associate them with cramped towns full of smoking chimneys. But the earliest mills were sited in surprisingly rural locations, often in the little steep-sided valleys known as cloughs, where fast-flowing becks and rivers could be dammed and diverted to turn the waterwheels. There are reminders, in wooded Newsholme Dean, that even a watercourse as small as Dean Beck could be harnessed to provide power to a cotton mill in Goose Eye. Weirs along the beck helped to maintain a good head of water, and one of the mill dams is now popular with anglers.

Laycock and Goose Eye

The village of Laycock contains a number of handsome old houses in the typical South Pennine style. While Laycock sits on the hillside, with good valley views, neighbouring Goose Eye nestles in a hollow. The village was originally called 'Goose Heights', which the local dialect contracted to 'Goose Ay', and thence to the name we know today. Lovers of real ale will already be familiar with the name, as this is the home of the Goose Eye Brewery.

WALK 40 DIRECTIONS

❶ Walk through the village of Laycock. Where the road narrows, go left down a paved track, Roberts Street. Beyond terraced houses, descend along a narrow walled path. You emerge on to a road, which you follow down into Goose Eye. Pass the Turkey Inn, the only pub on this walk. Just 50yds (46m) after you cross Dean Beck, take the steps on your right and re-cross the beck on a footbridge. Follow the beck upstream and take a footbridge on the right, across the channel of a now-dry mill leat.

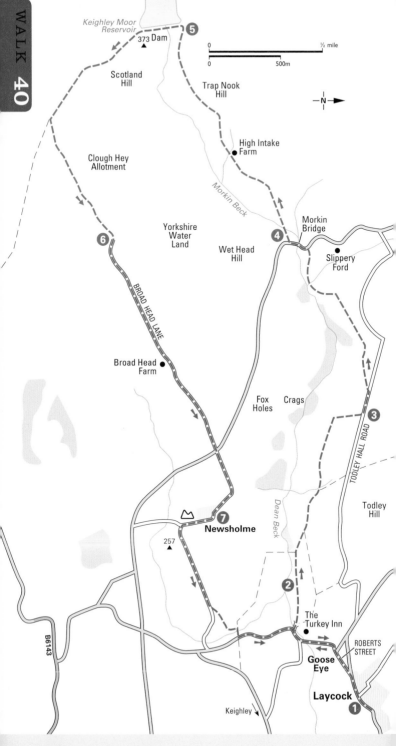

Keighley Moor Reservoir

373 Dam

Scotland Hill

Trap Nook Hill

5

½ mile

500m

—N→

High Intake Farm

Clough Hey Allotment

Morkin Beck

Yorkshire Water Land

Wet Head Hill

Morkin Bridge

4

Slippery Ford

6

BROAD HEAD LANE

Broad Head Farm

Fox Holes

Crags

3

TODLEY HALL ROAD

Todley Hill

Dean Beck

Newsholme

7

257

2

The Turkey Inn

ROBERTS STREET

B6143

Goose Eye

Keighley ↓

Laycock

1

② Pass a mill dam, soon enjoying easy walking, above the beck. Bear right at a fork, the path later levelling between pasture and scrubland. Pass the rear of a farmhouse, and cross a stony track, to continue in the same direction, via a gate, along a track (signed to Slippery Ford). Continue uphill, through another gate and across a stream to a choice of tracks. Keep right, up a hollow way (or the adjacent path). Your path, soon paved, goes through a gate and up to meet a road.

> **WHERE TO EAT AND DRINK**
> The Turkey Inn, towards the beginning of the walk in Goose Eye, is a splendid village pub, with a reputation for good food that extends much further afield.

③ Walk left, along the road, for 75yds (69m), before taking the access track on the left down to Bottoms Farm. Keep right of farm buildings to take a gate on the right. A path comes to a stile at the far end of a barn. Follow the path towards the head of the valley. Through a gate and then over stiles, the way continues across fields to pass below a farmhouse. At the bottom of the fourth field, two becks meet to form Dean Beck. Cross the beck in front of you, go through a gate and follow the other beck to a wall. Accompany the wall to the right, uphill, and take a gate on the left into the yard of Slitheroford Farm. Walk between some farm buildings and out to a road. Go left, down the road, and cross the beck once again at Morkin Bridge.

④ Turn immediately right through a gate on to Yorkshire Water land and follow a good metalled track uphill. You can lengthen your stride as the track traverses heather moorland, and passes a lonely farm, Higher Intake. The highest point of your walk is soon reached: Keighley Moor Reservoir.

⑤ Walk left, across the top of the dam. At the far end of the reservoir, ignore the signed track to the right and instead bear left at a concrete post along a gently descending moorland track. Reaching a boggy section keep ahead, the vague path eventually becoming more distinct as it joins a wall. Follow it for 150yds (137m) to a gateway, turn through and then bear half right to cross a line of grouse butts on a distinct but narrow path through the heather. Eventually, on meeting a track, follow it right over a cattle grid.

⑥ Soon leaving the moorland behind, Broad Head Lane becomes metalled beyond an isolated group of houses. Cross a road by a farm and continue on a track to Newsholme.

> **WHILE YOU'RE THERE**
> Visit Cliffe Castle Museum, set in an attractive hillside park on Spring Gardens Lane, Keighley. It was built in the 1880s as a mansion for a mill owner, and is now a museum, specialising in natural history and geology.

⑦ Wind between the houses and follow a lane down for 300 yards (274m). Opposite the entrance to a cottage, Green End Farm, turn left. Eventually degrading to a track, it later swings across a beck to meet a road. Walk left down into Goose Eye. Walk through the village and steeply up the road. From here, retrace your outward route back into Laycock.

Haworth's Brontë Moors

Across the wild Pennine moors to the
romantic ruin of Top Withins.

DISTANCE 7.5 miles (12.1km)	**MINIMUM TIME** 3hrs 30min
ASCENT/GRADIENT 968ft (295m) ▲▲▲	**LEVEL OF DIFFICULTY** +++
PATHS Well-signed and easy to follow, 1 stile	
LANDSCAPE Open moorland	
SUGGESTED MAP OS Explorer OL21 South Pennines	
START/FINISH Grid reference: SE 029372	
DOG FRIENDLINESS Under control near sheep on open moorland	
PARKING Pay-and-display car park, near Brontë Parsonage	
PUBLIC TOILETS Central Park, Haworth	

Who could have imagined, when the Revd Patrick Brontë became curate of the Church of St Michael and All Angels in 1820, that the little gritstone town of Haworth would become a literary Mecca to rival Grasmere and Stratford-upon-Avon? But it has, and visitors flock here in great numbers: some to gain some insights into the works of Charlotte, Emily and Anne, others just to enjoy a day out.

If the shy sisters could see the Haworth of today, they would recognise the steep, cobbled main street. But they would no doubt be amazed to see the tourist industry that's built up to exploit their names and literary reputations. They would recognise the Georgian parsonage too. Now a museum, it has been painstakingly restored to reflect the lives of the Brontës and the rooms are filled with their personal treasures.

That three such prodigious talents should be found within a single family is remarkable enough. To have created such towering works as *Jane Eyre* and *Wuthering Heights* while living in what was a bleakly inhospitable place is almost beyond belief. The public were unprepared for this trio of lady novelists, which is why all the books published during their lifetimes bore the androgynous pen-names of Currer, Ellis and Acton Bell.

From the day that Patrick Brontë came to Haworth with his wife and six children, tragedy was never far away. His wife died the following year and two daughters did not live to adulthood. His only son, Branwell, succumbed to drink and drugs; Anne and Emily died aged 29 and 30 respectively. Charlotte, alone, lived long enough to marry. But after just one year of marriage – to her father's curate – she too fell ill and died in 1855, at the age of 38. Revd Brontë survived them all, living to the ripe old age of 84.

Tourism is no recent development; by the middle of the 19th century, the first literary pilgrims were finding their way to Haworth. No matter how crowded this little town becomes (and those who value their solitude should avoid visiting on a sunny summer weekend), it is always possible to escape to the moors that surround the town. You can follow, literally, in the footsteps of the three sisters as they sought freedom and inspiration, away from the stifling confines of the parsonage and the adjacent graveyard.

HAWORTH

As you explore these inhospitable moors, you'll get a greater insight into the literary world of the Brontës than those who stray no further than the souvenir shops and tea rooms of Haworth.

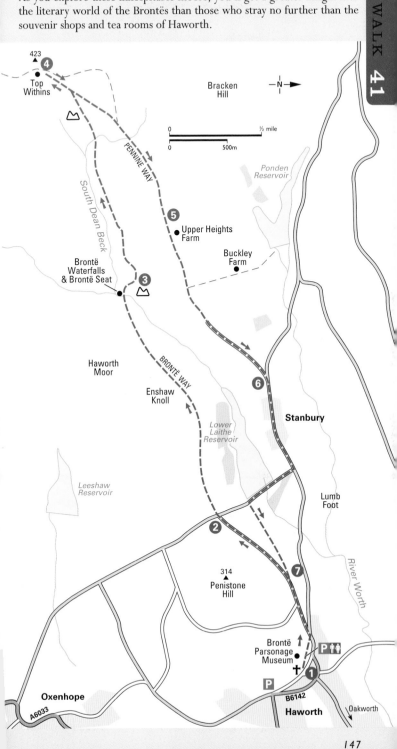

WALK 41 DIRECTIONS

1 Take the cobbled lane beside the King's Arms, signed to the Brontë Parsonage Museum. The lane soon becomes a paved field path that leads to the Haworth–Stanbury road. Walk left along the road and, after just 75yds (69m), take a left fork, signed to Penistone Hill. Continue along this quiet road to a T-junction.

2 Take the track straight ahead, soon signed 'Brontë Way and Top Withins', gradually descending to South Dean Beck where, within a few paces of the stone bridge, you'll find the Brontë Waterfalls and Brontë Seat (a stone that resembles a chair). Cross the bridge and climb steeply uphill to a three-way sign.

3 Keep left, uphill, on a paved path signed 'Top Withins'. The path levels out to accompany a wall. Cross a beck on stepping stones; a steep uphill climb brings you to a signpost by a ruined building. Walk a short distance left, uphill, to visit the ruin of Top Withins, possibly the inspiration for Wuthering Heights.

4 Retrace your steps to the signpost, but now keep ahead on a paved path, downhill, signed to Stanbury and Haworth and the Pennine Way. Follow a broad, clear track across the wide expanse of wild Pennine moorland.

5 Pass a white farmhouse – Upper Heights Farm – then bear immediately left at a fork of tracks (still signed here as the Pennine Way). Walk past another building, Lower Heights Farm. After 500yds (457m), you come to a crossing path: where the Pennine Way veers off to the left, you should continue on the track straight ahead, signed to Stanbury and Haworth. Follow the track to meet a road near the village of Stanbury.

6 Bear right along the road through Stanbury, then take the first road on the right, signed to Oxenhope, and cross the dam of Lower Laithe Reservoir. Immediately beyond the dam, turn left on a road that is soon reduced to a track uphill, to meet a road by Haworth Cemetery.

7 From here you retrace your outward route: walk left along the road, soon taking a gap stile on the right, to follow the paved field path back into Haworth.

Shipley Glen's Tramway and Baildon Moor

A glimpse of moorland and a traditional rural playground for the mill workers of Shipley and Saltaire.

DISTANCE 4 miles (6.4km)		**MINIMUM TIME** 2hrs	

ASCENT/GRADIENT 640ft (195m) ▲▲▲ **LEVEL OF DIFFICULTY** ✦✦✦

PATHS Moor and field paths, no stiles

LANDSCAPE Moorland, fields and gritstone rocks

SUGGESTED MAP OS Explorer 288 Bradford & Huddersfield

START/FINISH Grid reference: SE 131389

DOG FRIENDLINESS Can be off leads except in Saltaire

PARKING On Glen Road, between Bracken Hall Countryside Centre and Old Glen House pub

PUBLIC TOILETS At Bracken Hall Countryside Centre; also in Saltaire

For the people of Shipley and Saltaire, Baildon Moor has traditionally represented a taste of the countryside on their doorsteps. Mill-hands could leave the mills and cramped terraced streets behind, and breathe clean Pennine air. They could listen to the song of the skylark and the bubbling cry of the curlew. There were heather moors to tramp across, gritstone rocks to scramble up and, at Shipley Glen, springy sheep-grazed turf on which to spread out a picnic blanket. There was also a funfair to visit – not a small affair either but a veritable theme park.

Towards the end of the 19th century Shipley Glen was owned by a Colonel Maude, who created a number of attractions. Visitors could enjoy the sundry delights of the Switchback Railway, Marsden's Menagerie, the Horse Tramway and the Aerial Runway. More sedate pleasures could be found at the Camera Obscura, the boating lake in the Japanese garden, and the Temperance Tea Room and Coffee House.

Sam Wilson, a local entrepreneur, played his own part in developing Shipley Glen. In 1895 he created the Shipley Glen Tramway. Saltaire people could now stroll through Roberts Park, past the steely-gazed statue of Sir Titus Salt, and enjoy the tram-ride to the top of the glen. Thousands of people would clamber, each weekend, on to the little cable-hauled 'toast-rack' cars. As one car went up the hill, another car would descend on an adjacent track.

In commercial terms, the heyday of Shipley Glen was during the Edwardian era. On busy days, as many as 17,000 people would take the tramway up to the pleasure gardens. Losing out to more sophisticated entertainments, however, Shipley Glen went into a slow decline. Sadly, all the attractions are now gone, but you can still take the ride on the tramway – which runs every weekend and bank holiday afternoon throughout the year. There is an attractive souvenir shop at the top, while the bottom station houses a small museum and replica Edwardian shop.

The Old Glen House is still a popular pub, though the former Temperance Tea Room and Coffee House has been transformed into the Bracken Hall

SHIPLEY GLEN

Countryside Centre. Local people still enjoy the freedom of the heather moorland. Despite all the changes, Shipley Glen retains a stubbornly old-fashioned air, and is all the better for it.

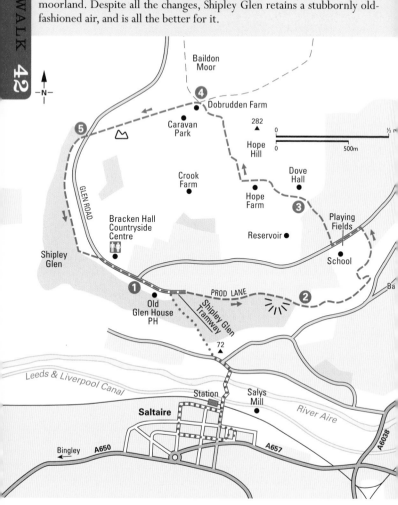

WALK 42 DIRECTIONS

① Walk down Glen Road, passing the Old Glen House pub. Continue as the road becomes Prod Lane, signed as a cul-de-sac. Where the road ends at the entrance to the Shipley Glen Tramway, keep straight ahead to locate an enclosed path to the right of a house. Follow this path, with houses on your left, and woodland to your right. As you come to a metal barrier, ignore a path to the left. Keep straight on

downhill. 100yds (91m) beyond the barrier, there is a choice of paths; bear left here, contouring the steep hillside and soon getting good views over Saltaire, Shipley and the Aire Valley.

② At a fork above a building, take the right branch, which undulates beneath a quarried sandstone cliff. When you later come to an area of open heath, with panoramic views, take a set of stone steps, with metal handrails, up to the top of the cliff. Turn right on a path between chain-link fences, which takes you around school playing fields, to meet a road. Walk left along the road for 150yds (137m). When you are level with the school on your left, cross the road and take a narrow, enclosed path on the right, between houses. Walk gradually uphill, crossing a road in a housing estate and picking up the enclosed path again. Soon, at a kissing gate, you emerge into pasture.

❸ Go half left, uphill, to a kissing gate at the top-left corner of the field. Head out to join an access track along the field top to Hope Farm. Walk past the buildings on a cinder track, leaving just before its end onto a bridleway through a gate on the right. Beyond the next gate you come out on to

Baildon Moor. Your path is clear, following a wall to your left. Keep straight on, as the wall curves to the left, towards the next farm (and caravan park). Cross a metalled farm track and curve left to follow the boundary wall of Dobrudden Farm.

❹ Walk gradually downhill towards Bingley in the valley. When the wall bears left, keep straight ahead, through bracken, more steeply downhill. Cross a metalled track and carry on down to meet Glen Road again.

❺ Follow the path along the rocky edge of wooded Shipley Glen, leading you back to the Bracken Hall Countryside Centre and your car.

EXTENDING THE WALK

The walk can be extended by taking the tramway or adjacent path down into the valley and exploring Salt's Mill and the model village of Saltaire.

Bingley and the St Ives Estate

*Great views of Airedale from
a viewpoint known as the Druid's Altar.*

DISTANCE **6 miles (9.7km)**   MINIMUM TIME **3hrs**

ASCENT/GRADIENT **853ft (260m)** ▲▲▲   LEVEL OF DIFFICULTY **+++**

PATHS **Good paths and tracks throughout, 1 stile**

LANDSCAPE **Woodland, park and river**

SUGGESTED MAP **OS Explorer 288 Bradford & Huddersfield**

START/FINISH **Grid reference: SE 107391**

DOG FRIENDLINESS **Can be off lead on St Ives Estate**

PARKING **Car parks in Bingley**

PUBLIC TOILETS **In Myrtle Park, Bingley**

Sitting astride both the River Aire and the Leeds and Liverpool Canal, in a steep-sided valley, Bingley is a typical West Yorkshire town. With its locks, wharves and plethora of mills, the town grew in size and importance during the 19th century as the textile trades expanded. But Bingley's pre-eminence did not begin with the Industrial Revolution; it is, in fact, one of the county's oldest settlements, with its market charter being granted by King John as far back as 1212.

In keeping with its age, Bingley has a number of splendid old buildings, such as the town hall, parish church, butter cross, the old market hall and the Old White Horse, a venerable coaching inn, where King John is reputed to have stayed. Ancient and modern sit side-by-side in Bingley, which has more than its fair share of more recent architectural monstrosities (look out for the headquarters of the Bradford & Bingley Building Society).

Halliwell Sutcliffe, author of such books as *The Striding Dales* and *By Moor and Fell*, lived in Bingley while his father was headmaster of the town's Grammar School.

River Aire

The River Aire rises close to the village of Malham, in the limestone dales of North Yorkshire, and flows past Bingley. By the time it joins the Ouse and decants into the Humber Estuary, it has been one of the hardest worked watercourses in Yorkshire. When the textile trades were at their height, the Aire was both a source of power for the woollen mills and a convenient dumping ground for industrial waste. But, like so many other West Yorkshire rivers, the water quality is now greatly improved.

St Ives

For part of this walk, you will be exploring the St Ives Estate, which from 1636 was owned by one of Bingley's most prominent families, the Ferrands. It was William Ferrand who, during the 1850s, landscaped the estate and created many of the paths and tracks that climb steeply up through the woods. The view from the top of the hill is ample reward for your efforts.

BINGLEY

From the gritstone outcrop known – somewhat fancifully – as the Druid's Altar, you have a splendid panorama across Bingley and the Aire Valley.

There is an inscription on Lady Blantyre's Rock, passed later on this walk, which commemorates William Ferrand's mother-in-law. Lady Blantyre often used to sit in the shade of this rock and read a book. A splendid notion: a monument to idleness. Near by is an obelisk with a dedication to William Ferrand himself. St Ives, a little wooded oasis on Bingley's doorstep, is now looked after by Bradford Council on behalf of local people.

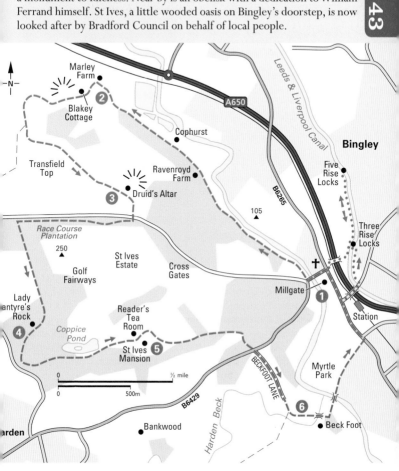

WALK 43 DIRECTIONS

❶ Walk downhill from the centre of Bingley, towards the church. Go left at the traffic lights, passing the Old White Horse pub, on to Millgate. Cross the River Aire and take the first right, Ireland Street. Swing immediately right and then left to join a riverside track. Very soon you seem to have swapped town for country. Bear right in front of Ravenroyd Farm, to pass between other farm buildings and continue on a walled track. Pass another house, Cophurst, and carry on through successive pastures beside a wood.

❷ Leaving the trees, the ongoing track continues past Marley Farm to end over a stile and stream onto a track by Blakey Cottage. Go left, bypassing a ford to follow the rough track uphill. As it later swings into a farm, bear right on a grass trail that winds up the bracken-clad slope, ultimately arriving at a small gate into thicker woodland. A narrow path rises on through the trees. Bear right and then left at successive forks to reach level ground at the top of the wood beside a wall running on your right. Eventually, after crossing a track, the path leads to a rocky outcrop, known as the Druid's Altar, with splendid views.

> **WHAT TO LOOK OUT FOR**
>
> Having been removed from the main street, Bingley's ancient stocks, butter cross and old market hall were re-sited near to the Ferrands Arms and the entrance to Myrtle Park.

❸ Bear right, after the rocks, to a meeting of tracks. Go through a gap in the wall opposite, on to a walled track into the St Ives Estate. Leave immediately through a kissing gate on the right onto a path that runs for 0.5 mile (800m) within Race Course Plantation. Ignoring the kissing gate leading out at the end, go left, now descending, initially still within trees through a golf course and then at the edge of open heather moor. When the accompanying wall later turns away, bear right with the main path, dropping through wood once more to come upon Lady Blantyre's Rock.

❹ Ignoring side-tracks, follow the path downhill, past exuberant displays of rhododendrons, to Coppice Pond. Join a metalled road to bear left, soon passing Reader's Tea Room, the golf clubhouse and then, set back on the right, the house itself, St Ives Mansion.

❺ Beyond the house, curve right and left to follow the main drive downhill for 0.5 mile (800m). Just after passing a car park, take

> **WHERE TO EAT AND DRINK**
>
> With 12th-century origins, the Old White Horse Inn is Bingley's oldest pub and housed the court, police cells and gibbet. Serving food at weekends, it has oodles of character. At St Ives, try Reader's Tea Room, for hot and cold snacks all day.

a path, left, into woodland. Keep right where it immediately forks, to reach the B6429, the Bingley to Cullingworth road. Cross it and continue downhill on narrow Beckfoot Lane. After houses the lane becomes an unmade track leading down to a delectable spot: here you will find Beckfoot Farm, in a wooded setting by Harden Beck, with a ford and an old packhorse bridge that dates back to 1723.

❻ Cross the bridge and bear left at Beckfoot Farm, to find allotments on your left. Where the allotments end, take a path to the left which leads to a metal footbridge over the River Aire and into Myrtle Park. Walk ahead through the park to arrive once again in the centre of Bingley.

EXTENDING THE WALK

The main walk can be extended to include a visit to Bingley's famous 'staircase' of locks. Return along the tow path to the Three Rise Locks and turn right across a footbridge that spans the bypass and railway line. It leads back to the main road near the parish church.

> **WHILE YOU'RE THERE**
>
> South of Bingley is the little town of Cottingley where, in 1917, two young girls took photographs of fairies by Cottingley Beck. Despite the fairies looking like paper cut-outs, the pictures were 'authenticated' by Arthur Conan Doyle, creator of the fiercely logical Sherlock Holmes.

Oxenhope and the Worth Valley Railway

*A moorland round and
a return to the age of steam.*

DISTANCE 6.5 miles (10.4km)   **MINIMUM TIME** 3hrs 30min

ASCENT/GRADIENT 1,115ft (340m) ▲▲▲   **LEVEL OF DIFFICULTY** +++

PATHS *Good paths and tracks, 6 stiles*

LANDSCAPE *Upland scenery, moor and pasture*

SUGGESTED MAP *OS Explorer OL21 South Pennines*

START/FINISH *Grid reference: SE 032353*

DOG FRIENDLINESS *Keep on lead along country lanes*

PARKING *Street parking in Oxenhope, near Keighley and Worth Valley Railway station*

PUBLIC TOILETS *None en route*

Oxenhope is at the end of the line in more ways than one. As well as being the terminus of the Keighley and Worth Valley Railway, Oxenhope is the last village in the Worth Valley. To the north are Haworth and Keighley; going south, into Calderdale and Hebden Bridge, requires you to gear down for a scenic drive over the lonely heights of Cock Hill.

Oxenhope was a farming community that expanded with the textile industry. The mills, however, have mostly disappeared, leaving the village to commuters who work in nearby towns. Apart from the railway, the village is best known for the Oxenhope Straw Race, held each year on the first Sunday in July. Competitors have to carry a bale of straw around the village, while drinking as much beer as possible. Whoever finishes this assault course first, it is the local charities that benefit most.

Keighley and Worth Valley Railway

The Keighley and Worth Valley line, running for 5 miles (8km) from Keighley to Oxenhope, is one of the longest established private railways in the country, and the last remaining complete branch line. It was built in 1867, funded by local mill owners, but the trains were run by the Midland Railway to link to the main Leeds–Skipton line at Keighley.

When the line fell victim to Dr Beeching's axe in 1962, local rail enthusiasts banded together in opposition to the closure. The preservation society bought the line: a pioneering example of rail privatisation. Thus began a major restoration of the line and the stations. Ingrow station, for example, had been so badly vandalised that a complete station was 'trainsported' to the site stone by stone from Foulridge in Lancashire. Built to the typical Midland style, it blends in well with the other stations on the line.

By 1968 the society began running a regular timetable of trains that has continued ever since. Steam trains run every weekend throughout the year, and daily in summer. But the line doesn't just cater for tourists; locals in the Worth Valley appreciate the diesel services into Keighley which operate on almost 200 days per year.

OXENHOPE

The line runs through the heart of Brontë country, with stations at Oxenhope, Haworth, Oakworth, Danems, Ingrow and Keighley. The stations are a particular delight: fully restored, gas-lit and redolent of the age of steam. So when Edith Nesbitt's classic children's novel, *The Railway Children*, was being filmed in 1970, the Keighley and Worth Valley Railway was a natural choice of setting. Oakworth station – a splendid example of an Edwardian station, complete with enamel advertising signs – is the one used in the film.

WALK 44 DIRECTIONS

1 Begin along the minor lane beside the entrance of Oxenhope Station, which leads up to the A6033. Cross the road and take Dark Lane ahead, a sunken lane that goes steeply uphill. Follow this track to a road. Go right here, downhill, to join the Denholme road (B6141). Walk left along the road, up to the Dog and Gun pub, where you turn right on to Sawood Lane.

2 At Coblin Farm, your route becomes a rough track. Through a gate at the end, join a metalled road and go right, signed 'Brontë Way'. After 100yds (91m), when the road accesses Thornton Moor Reservoir, walk straight ahead through a gate on an unmade track, ignoring the Brontë Way which leaves shortly on the right.

3 At a fork, just 50yds (46m) further on, keep right as the track goes downhill, curving towards a transmission mast in the middle distance. Pass a clump of trees, and cross a watercourse before descending to a minor road.

4 Go right here, eventually passing a cattle grid and the mast. 150yds (137m) beyond the mast, as the road begins a steep descent, take a wall stile on the left. Later, through another wall stile, walk

left, uphill, on a broad, walled track that deposits you at the Waggon & Horses Inn.

5 Walk left for some 30yds (27m) and cross to a signed track that drops steeply downhill. Levelling after 300yds (274m), it swings right. Take a stile to the left, by a gate. Bearing from the wall, carry on downhill crossing successive stiles to meet a walled path at the bottom. Go left here, cross a stream, and continue uphill to arrive at the entrance to Lowerfold Farm.

6 Follow the farm track to the right; turn right again, 20yds (18m) further on, at the end of a cottage, to join a metalled track. The track soon bears right above Leeshaw Reservoir and makes a gradual descent. Pass a mill to meet a road.

7 Cross the road and take the track ahead (signed to Marsh). Keep right of the first house, on a narrow walled path and continue across a small field. Through a courtyard, go left and right past cottages. Emerging, take the kissing gate opposite, from which a path runs through to a walled track. To the right it leads past houses and then across a field, finally ending at a road. Go right, back down into Oxenhope.

Discovering the Rural Side of Leeds

*From the bustle of the city
to the heart of the country.*

DISTANCE 5 miles (8km)	MINIMUM TIME 2hrs 30min
ASCENT/GRADIENT 541 feet (165m) ▲▲▲	LEVEL OF DIFFICULTY +++

PATHS Urban ginnels, parkland and woodland paths, 2 stiles

LANDSCAPE Mostly woodland

SUGGESTED MAP OS Explorers 289 Leeds, 297 Lower Wharfedale

START Grid reference: SE 293350 (on Explorer 289)

FINISH Grid reference: SE 270402 (on Explorer 297)

DOG FRIENDLINESS Good, but watch for traffic early on

PARKING Street parking around Raglan Road off the A660, opposite Hyde Park

PUBLIC TOILETS Meanwood Park

This, the only linear walk in the book, is a splendid ramble, surprisingly rural in aspect throughout, even though it begins just a stone's throw from the bustling heart of Leeds. You start among the terraces of red-brick houses that are so typical of the city, and five minutes later you are in delightful woodland.

Linking with the Dales Way

The walk follows the first 5 miles (8km) of the Dales Way link path from Leeds to Ilkley (the walk's official starting point). This link path begins at Woodhouse Moor — where fairs and circuses have long pitched their tents — so we shall do the same. The path follows Woodhouse Ridge into Meanwood Park and along the Meanwood Valley, cocooned against creeping suburbia by a slim sliver of woodland. The route is also promoted as the Meanwood Valley Trail, so there are regular waymarkers to keep you on track.

Parklife

Leeds is fortunate to have so many parks within the city limits: long-established green spaces such as Roundhay Park, and newer parks created from 'brownfield' sites. The first few miles of this walk are through some of this pleasant parkland. Then, having crossed beneath the Leeds Ring Road, you have the more natural surroundings of Adel Woods to enjoy.

The walk finishes near Adel church, dedicated to St John the Baptist. Though small, it is one of the most perfectly proportioned Norman churches in the country, having been built about 1170. The ornamental stone carving is noteworthy — especially the four arches framing the doorway. From Adel, there's a reliable bus service back to Woodhouse Moor. To lengthen the walk by 1.5 miles (2.4km), don't turn left down Stair Foot Lane (at Point **Ⓐ**), but take the track ahead, and turn left when you come to King Lane. This will bring you out at Golden Acre Park, near Bramhope (on the same bus route for getting back to Leeds).

MEANWOOD VALLEY

Golden Acre Park

Eccup Reservoir

KING LANE

Adel Dam

A660

OTELEY ROAD

½ mile
500m

DALES WAY

Adel Church

BACK CHURCH LANE

6 ✝

STAIR FOOT LN

A

Rugby Ground

Lawnswood Arms

Adel

Adel Beck

5

120 ▲
Dunstarn Farm

Boddington Hall

A6120

A6120

4

A61

Meanwood Park

B6157

Carr Manor

3

Unisversity

Mill

2

Beckett Park

B6159

Meanwood Valley Farm

Meanwood Beck

B6157

Leeds

DALES WAY

Headingley Cricket Ground

A660

WOODHOUSE STREET

DELPH LN

Woodhouse Carr

A61

Burley Park Station

Burley

Hyde Park

RAGLAN ROAD

1

A65

A58

WALK 45

WALK 45 DIRECTIONS

① Walk down Raglan Road (opposite the library at the corner of Hyde Park) and turn right on to Rampart Road. Cross Woodhouse Street, and walk ahead up Delph Lane. When the road finally ends, take a gate and walk left on the higher path along Woodhouse Ridge. Keep with the main trail to a barrier. Where it then splits, take the middle option, signed to Grove Road. There, follow the continuing path opposite, which shortly emerges at Monkbridge Road.

② Cross the road and take Highbury Lane, keeping ahead beyond to recover the path, which now accompanies Meanwood Beck. As you pass a mill, follow a path first left, then right, above the mill dam. Walk between allotments and out to join a road for just 100yds (91m). Turn right, in front of a post box, through stone gate-posts, to enter Meanwood Park. Beyond a small car park, go sharp left on a metalled lane through the park, to a short row of terraced houses known as Hustlers Row.

③ Keep left of the houses as the lane becomes a stony track. Cross Meanwood Beck on a footbridge, bearing right at a fork of tracks to follow the beck into woodland. Cross an outflow on to the raised bank of a mill leat and follow it right above the beck. Ignore side-tracks and a footbridge on the left to arrive at a double bridge by a weir. Cross the beck to your right, and continue to follow its course. Some 50yds (46m) beyond the bridge, just before a stile, go right and immediately left to follow a field-edge path. Meet a road by a picnic site and information panel. Go left along the road. Just 20yds (18m) from the ring road, go right on a metalled track which soon continues as a path. Beyond a paddock go left through a tunnel beneath the road.

④ Take steps, at the far end, on to a path that follows Adel Beck. Keep left of the next pile of boulders, rising to a path along the fringe of the woodland. Keep to this higher path until you eventually reach a major fork. Bear right, following an aqueduct across the dip of the valley. Curving left, the path continues through Adel Woods, in time meeting a prominent junction.

⑤ The Meanwood Valley Trail is signed left, dropping across a stone slab bridge and climbing steps to a small pond. There, fork right, soon passing the corner of a rugby ground. Beyond a picnic area, the main path bears left, emerging through a car park on to Stair Foot Lane. Go left down the road; this sunken lane soon rises to a junction. Go right on to Back Church Lane. When the road bears right, keep ahead along a path that takes you straight to Adel church.

⑥ Walk past the church and leave the churchyard by a collection of coffins and millstones. Cross the road and take a field path opposite. Bear half left across the next field to the Otley Road (A660). Turn left to find a bus stop, opposite the Lawnswood Arms, for the bus back to Woodhouse Moor, in Leeds.

WHERE TO EAT AND DRINK

There are several pubs just off-route during this walk. But the simplest option is to wait until the finishing point, where you will find the Lawnswood Arms. Your car is parked close to the university, so you will find cheap and cheerful curry houses nearby, and some characterful city pubs.

Jumble Hole and Colden Clough

Textile history from cottage industry to the mills of bustling Hebden Bridge.

DISTANCE 6 miles (9.7km)	**MINIMUM TIME** 3hrs
ASCENT/GRADIENT 1,132ft (345m) ▲▲▲	**LEVEL OF DIFFICULTY** ✦✦✦

PATHS Good paths, 14 stiles

LANDSCAPE Steep-sided valleys, fields and woodland

SUGGESTED MAP OS Explorer OL21 South Pennines

START/FINISH Grid reference: SD 991271

DOG FRIENDLINESS Good most of the way, but livestock in upland fields

PARKING Pay-and-display car parks in Hebden Bridge

PUBLIC TOILETS Hebden Bridge and Heptonstall

This walk links the little town of Hebden Bridge with the old hand-weaving village of Heptonstall, using sections of a waymarked walk, the Calderdale Way. The hill village of Heptonstall is by far the older settlement and was, in its time, an important centre of the textile trade. A cursory look at a map shows Heptonstall to be at the hub of a complex network of old trackways, mostly used by packhorse trains carrying wool and cotton. And Heptonstall's Cloth Hall, where cloth was bought and sold, dates back to the 16th century. At this time, Hebden Bridge was little more than a river crossing on an old packhorse causey.

Wheels of Industry

Heptonstall's importance came at the time when textiles were, literally, a cottage industry, with spinning and weaving being undertaken in isolated farmhouses. When the processes began to be mechanised, during the Industrial Revolution, Heptonstall, with no running water to power the waterwheels, was left high and dry. As soon as spinning and weaving developed on a truly industrial scale, communities sprang up wherever there was a ready supply of running water. So the town of Hebden Bridge was established in the valley, at the meeting of two rivers: the Calder and Hebden Water. The handsome 16th-century packhorse bridge that gives the town its name still spans Hebden Water.

At one time there were more than 30 mills in Hebden Bridge, their tall chimneys belching thick smoke into the Calder Valley. It used to be said that the only time you could see the town from the surrounding hills was during Wakes Week, the mill-hands' traditional holiday. The town's speciality was cotton: mostly hard-wearing fustian and corduroy. With Hebden Bridge being hemmed in by hills, and the mills occupying much of the available land on the valley bottom, the workers' houses had to be built up the steep slopes. An ingenious solution to the problem was to build 'top and bottom' houses, one dwelling on top of another. They can be viewed to best effect on the last leg of the walk, which offers a stunning birds-eye view over the town.

HEBDEN BRIDGE

Few looms clatter today and Hebden Bridge has reinvented itself as the 'capital' of Upper Calderdale, as a place to enjoy a day out. The town is known for its excellent walking country, bohemian population, trips along the Rochdale Canal by horse-drawn narrowboats and its summer arts festival. Jumble Hole Clough is a typical South Pennine steep-sided, wooded valley. Though a tranquil scene today, this little valley was once a centre of industry, with four mills exploiting the fast-flowing beck as it makes its way down to join the River Calder. You can see remains of all these mills, and some of their mill ponds, on this walk; but the most intriguing relic is Staups Mill, now an evocative ruin, near the top of Jumble Hole Clough.

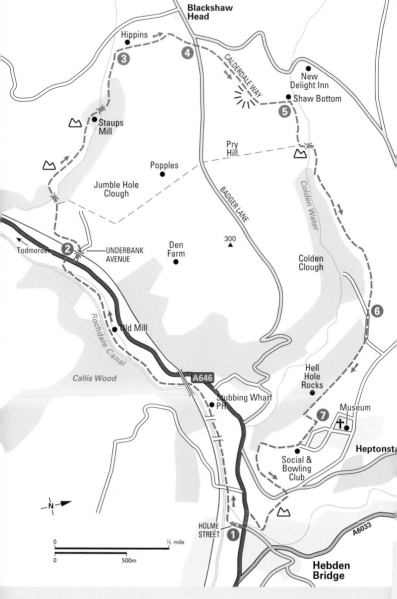

HEBDEN BRIDGE

WALK 46 DIRECTIONS

1 Begin along Holme Street, off the main A646 just west of the park, to the Rochdale Canal. Go right to follow the tow path beneath two bridges, past the Stubbing Wharf pub and beneath a railway bridge. Carry on for another 0.75 mile (1.2km) before turning off before the next bridge to follow a track to the A646.

2 Cross the road and turn right for just 75yds (69m) to take Underbank Avenue, on the left. Walk beneath the railway and go left again, past houses, to where another road comes through the viaduct. Go right on a track past a mill, and follow the beck up into the woodland of Jumble Hole Clough. Where the track later swings sharp right, leave across a stone bridge on to a track rising steeply through a hairpin. Higher up as it wheels left, take the narrow path ahead. Continue above the beck, eventually intersecting a path, which drops right to Staups Mill. The climb resumes beyond the ruin to reach a footbridge. Scale the opposite bank and go left in front of a signpost by a gap in a wall to come out at Hippins.

3 Join the Calderdale Way, turning right up a track between farm buildings to a stile. Follow a path to the next stile; then between a fence and a wall. Cross the track to Apple Tree Farm, to follow a line of causeway stones across three more stiles, passing to the right of a cottage. Cross the field to a gate at the far side, then follow a causeway over a stile, and along a track to the lane at Blackshaw Head.

4 Cross to a small gate almost opposite and bear half right across the field to a stile, then follow the right edge of the next field. Continue on a diagonal line across successive fields, eventually reaching a walled track. Walk down to Shaw Bottom and bear left beside the house to a junction.

5 The New Delight Inn is to the left, but the route lies to the right. Keep ahead as the way degrades to a stony track. After 200yds (183m), bear left beside a waypost on a stepped path dropping steeply to a bridge across Colden Water. Climb up the other side, forking right to follow a causeway at the top of woodland. Carry on as you later break out into a field. Over a stile at the far corner, pass in front of the adjacent gate to a second stile and pick up the continuing flagged path. Eventually meeting a rising track, go left to a junction and turn right on a tarmac drive. Approaching a house, stay ahead on a path behind it, which shortly meets an intersecting walled track. Follow it right to a lane at its end.

6 Walk up the hill, leaving just before a bend through a gap in the right-hand wall. From here your path meanders through woodland (it's a bit of a scramble in places). Emerge from the woodland, and follow a wall to Hell Hole Rocks. Beyond the outcrop, turn away from the edge along a walled path. Cross an access road and continue behind houses to a junction.

7 To visit Heptonstall bear left and follow Walk 49. Otherwise, go right behind more houses to the Social and Bowling Club. There, turn right on a contained path, curving left beyond the wall's end. Later dropping into trees, join a path from the right. Meeting a track, turn right to a road junction. Bear left along the lower, main road, doubling sharply right after 50yds (46m) onto an old packhorse road, the Buttress, which drops steeply back into Hebden Bridge.

The Bridestone Rocks from Lydgate

Ancient tracks and gritstone outcrops,
with terrific views of the steep-sided Cliviger Valley.

DISTANCE 6 miles (9.7km)	**MINIMUM TIME** 3hrs
ASCENT/GRADIENT 1,296ft (395m) ▲▲▲	**LEVEL OF DIFFICULTY** +++

PATHS Moorland and packhorse paths, some quiet roads, 2 stiles

LANDSCAPE Steep-sided valley and open moorland

SUGGESTED MAP OS Explorer OL21 South Pennines

START/FINISH Grid reference: SD 923255

DOG FRIENDLINESS Be careful around sheep grazing on the moorland

PARKING Roadside parking in Lydgate, 1.5 miles (2.4km) out of Todmorden, on A646, signposted to Burnley

PUBLIC TOILETS None en route

The Long Causeway, between Halifax and Burnley, is an ancient trading route, possibly dating back to the Bronze Age. Crosses and waymarker stones helped to guide travellers across the moorland wastes, though most of them have been lost or damaged in the intervening years. Amazingly, Mount Cross has survived intact: a splendid, though crudely carved, example of the Celtic 'wheel-head' design. Opinions differ about its age but it is certainly the oldest man-made artefact in the area, erected at least a thousand years ago.

The Sportsmans Arms, visited on this walk, is one of many isolated pubs in the South Pennines that seem to be situated 'miles from anywhere'. In fact they were built on old routes, and catered for customers on the move, such as drovers and the men who led the trains of packhorse ponies across the moorland tracks. The Sportsmans Arms lies on the Long Causeway, now upgraded to a high-level road between Todmorden and Burnley. These days the pub caters for motorists and walkers, with good food and beers.

The Bridestones

The hills and moors to the north of Todmorden are dotted with gritstone outcrops. The impressive piles of Orchan Rocks and Whirlaw Stones are both encountered on this walk. But the most intriguing rock formations are to be found at the Bridestones. One rock in particular has been weathered by wind and water into a tear-drop shape, and stands on a base that looks far too slender to support its great weight. It resembles a rock in the North York Moors National Park, which is also known as the Bridestone.

Cliviger Valley

The Cliviger Valley links two towns – Todmorden in West Yorkshire and Burnley in Lancashire – that expanded with the textile trade, and then suffered when that trade went into decline. The valley itself is narrow and steep-sided, in places almost a gorge. Into the cramped confines of the valley are shoe-horned the road, railway line, the infant River Calder and communities such as Portsmouth, Cornholme and Lydgate that grew up around the textile mills. The mills were powered by fast-flowing becks, running off the steep hillsides. The valley is almost a microcosm of the Industrial Revolution: by no means beautiful, but full of character. This area is particularly well provided with good footpaths, some of them still paved with their original causey stones.

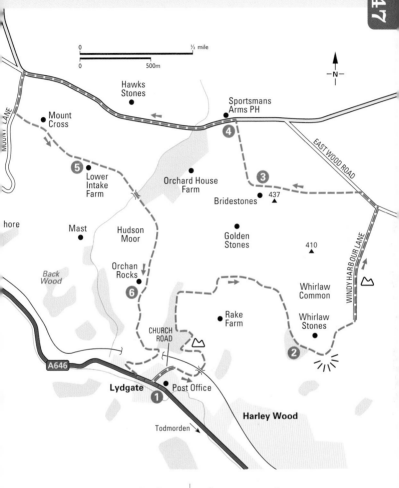

WALK 47 DIRECTIONS

1 From the post office in Lydgate, take Church Road. At the end, go right along Owlers Walk, immediately bearing off right on a contained path. Meeting a track at its end, follow it beneath a railway bridge and up to Stannally Farm. The onward track zig-zags steeply up the wooded hillside, eventually breaking onto the edge of open moor where it swings right towards a farm. Keep left of the farmhouse, continuing along a walled track uphill. When you meet another walled track, go right towards a rocky outcrop on the first horizon. Beyond two gates you are on open moorland again: Whirlaw Common. Cross rough pasture on a section of paved causeway to arrive, via a gate, at Whirlaw Stones.

WALK 47

② Keep to the causeway that bears right, below the stones, with panoramic views of the Cliviger Valley, Todmorden and, ahead, Stoodley Pike. Leave Whirlaw Common by a gate on to a walled path. Turn sharp left opposite a farm, on a stony track that follows a wall uphill. Bear right around the rocks, to join Windy Harbour Lane. You have a steep climb, before the road levels off to meet Eastwood Road. Go left here for just 150yds (137m). Where the wall ends, take a kissing gate on the left. A grassy path leads you to another fascinating collection of rocks, known as the Bridestones.

③ Continue past the Bridestones through a landscape of scattered boulders. Beyond the trig point, keep ahead to cross a broken wall, just beyond which is a waypost beside the ruin of a second wall. Follow it right to emerge onto a lane opposite the Sportsmans Arms.

④ Go left, along the road; you have 1 mile (1.6km) of level walking, passing the Hawks Stones on the right and a handful of houses, until you come to a minor road on the left. This is Mount Lane, signed to Shore and Todmorden. Walk down for

WHERE TO EAT AND DRINK

The Sportsmans Arms is directly on the route of this walk. Better yet, it specialises in good food, as these isolated Pennine pubs now tend to do. The Staff of Life, on the main A646 at Lydgate, is another cosy 'real ale' pub where walkers get a warm welcome.

300yds (274m) before turning left onto a broad bridleway. Look out for Mount Cross, which stands a short way along, over the wall in a field to your left.

⑤ Bear left in front of Lower Intake Farm on a path that soon develops as a track. Cross an intersecting track and, later, a bridge spanning a stream before reaching a stile on the right. Ignore it, but take the adjacent track, which drops alongside a wall past another gritstone outcrop, Orchan Rocks.

WHILE YOU'RE THERE

If you continue along the Long Causeway, you'll soon come to Coal Clough Windfarm. These huge wind turbines can be found on the crest of many South Pennine hills, attracting strong winds and equally strong opinions. To some people they represent a sustainable future for energy, to others they are ugly intrusions in the landscape.

⑥ Where the wall bears left, beyond the rocks, follow it downhill to a stile. You now join a farm track that makes a serpentine descent through woodland back to Lydgate. Reaching the former Board School, now a nursery, turn sharp left back to the main road.

WHAT TO LOOK OUT FOR

In geological terms, the South Pennines are largely made up of Millstone grit and coarse sandstone. Where the gritstone is visible, it forms rocky crags and outcrops, like those encountered on this walk. The typical landscape is moorland of heather and peat, riven by steep-sided valleys. Here, in the cramped confines of the steep-sided Cliviger Valley, road, rail and river cross and re-cross each other – like the flex of an old-fashioned telephone.

Along Langfield Edge to Stoodley Pike

A classic South Pennine ridge walk
to a much-loved landmark.

DISTANCE *8.5 miles (13.7km)*   **MINIMUM TIME** *4hrs 30min*

ASCENT/GRADIENT *1,312ft (400m)* ▲▲▲   **LEVEL OF DIFFICULTY** +++

PATHS *Good paths and tracks, 2 stiles*

LANDSCAPE *Open moorland*

SUGGESTED MAP *OS Explorer OL21 South Pennines*

START/FINISH *Grid reference: SD 936241*

DOG FRIENDLINESS *Under control as sheep present throughout*

PARKING *Car parks in centre of Todmorden*

PUBLIC TOILETS *By bus station in Todmorden*

Todmorden – call it 'Tod' if you want to sound like a local – is a border town, standing at the junction of three valley routes. Before the town was included in the old West Riding, the Yorkshire/Lancashire border divided the town in two. Todmorden's splendid town hall, built in an unrestrained classical Greek style, reflects this dual personality. On top of the town hall are carved figures which represent, on one side, the Lancashire cotton trade, and, on the other side, Yorkshire agriculture and engineering.

Stoodley Pike

Stoodley Pike is a ubiquitous sight around the Calder Valley, an unmistakable landmark. It seems you only need to turn a corner, or crest a hill, and it appears on the horizon. West Yorkshire is full of monuments built on prominent outcrops, but few of them dominate the view in quite the way that Stoodley Pike does.

In 1814, a trio of patriotic Todmorden men convened in a local pub, the Golden Lion. Now that the Napoleonic War was over, they wanted to commemorate the peace with a suitably grand monument. So they organised a public subscription, and raised enough money to erect a monument, 1,476ft (450m) up on Langfield Edge, overlooking the town. Construction was halted, briefly, when Napoleon rallied his troops, and was not completed until the following year, when he was finally defeated at the Battle of Waterloo. This original monument was undone by the Pennine weather. Ironically, it collapsed in 1854, on the very day that the Crimean War broke out. Another group of local worthies came together (yes, at the Golden Lion again) to raise more money. So the Stoodley Pike we see today is Mark II: 131ft (40m) high and built to commemorate the ending of hostilities in the Crimea.

Stoodley Pike remains visible for almost every step of this exhilarating ridge walk. As well as being a favourite destination for local walkers, the Pike is visited by walkers on the Pennine Way. Remember to pack a torch for this walk. By climbing a flight of unlit stone steps inside the monument, you emerge at a viewing platform offering panoramic views over Calderdale and beyond.

STOODLEY PIKE

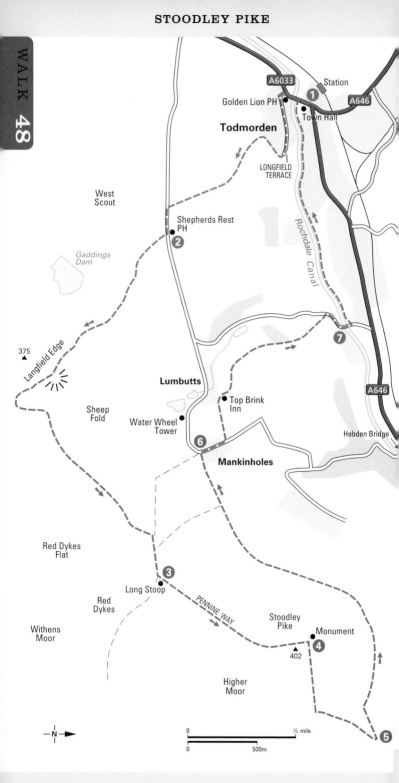

A6033

Station

Golden Lion PH

A646

Town Hall

Todmorden

LONGFIELD
TERRACE

West
Scout

Shepherds Rest
PH

2

*Gaddings
Dam*

Rochdale Canal

375
▲

Langfield Edge

7

Lumbutts

Top Brink
Inn

Sheep
Fold

Water Wheel
Tower

6

Hebden Bridge

A646

Mankinholes

Red Dykes
Flat

Long Stoop

3

PENNINE WAY

Stoodley
Pike

Monument

4

402
▲

Red
Dykes

Withens
Moor

Higher
Moor

—N—►

5

0   ½ mile

0   500m

STOODLEY PIKE

WALK 48 DIRECTIONS

1 From the town hall in the centre of Todmorden, take the Rochdale road (A6033), cross the canal, turning left and immediately left again around the Golden Lion pub to walk up Longfield Road. Keep ahead as the main street veers away to new houses, but then swing right with Longfield Road. At the top of the hill, the road peters out at Longfield Terrace. Take a track to the left, to find yourself suddenly 'on the tops'. When the track forks, keep left to a farm, from where you will get the first glimpse of your destination – Stoodley Pike – on the horizon ahead. Continue along the farm track to a road. Go left, to find a pub, the Shepherds Rest.

WHERE TO EAT AND DRINK

The isolated Shepherds Rest is near the beginning of the walk, while the Top Brink Inn at Lumbutts is towards the end. If you want to sit in the pub where the raising of Stoodley Pike was first discussed, you must wait till you have finished the walk: the Golden Lion is in Todmorden, close to the canal.

2 Opposite the pub, take a track leading through a gate, uphill, onto Langfield Common. Keep ahead past a waymark along a distinct and well-graded path that rises across the steep hillside below Langfield Edge. Levelling at the top, it is joined by another path to round the head of the clough. The way runs on above the edge, eventually intersecting a broader path. Go left towards the distant monument.

3 Later, rising from a dip, branch left at a minor fork and, ignoring the crossing of Calderdale Way, carry on past an ancient marker stone, Long Stoop, to Stoodley Pike, 0.75 mile (1.2km) further on.

4 From the monument, swing right, walking down to a wall stile. After a few paces cross a second stile in the adjacent wall, from which the path drops more steeply to a lower track, London Road.

5 Follow the track left in a long and gentle descent to come out onto a lane. Go right, into the hamlet of Mankinholes.

6 About 100yds (91m) beyond the last house, take a paved, walled track on the left, signed 'Pennine Bridleway', that emerges at the Top Brink Inn in another tiny settlement, Lumbutts. Turn right to take a path between houses and follow a section of causeway path at the field edge. At a gap stile in a wall, head right, slightly uphill, across a field to another gap stile. Now descending across the hillside and later becoming contained, the path ends at a farm track. Continue downhill to meet a minor road by cottages. Go right, passing a converted mill, to cross the Rochdale Canal.

7 Drop right to the tow path and follow the canal back under the bridge into the centre of Todmorden.

WHAT TO LOOK OUT FOR

London Road, the fancifully named track you follow from Stoodley Pike down into Mankinholes, was a 'cotton famine road'. When the cotton trade suffered one of its periodic slumps, mill owner John Fielden put some of his men to work on building this road, so he could ride his carriage up to Stoodley Pike. Fielden also built Dobroyd Castle, its castellated turrets looking slightly out of place on a hill overlooking the town.

Hardcastle Crags & Crimsworth Dean

A pair of beautiful wooded valleys, linked by a high level path.

WALK 49

DISTANCE 5 miles (8km)	MINIMUM TIME 2hrs 30min
ASCENT/GRADIENT 935ft (285m) ▲▲▲	LEVEL OF DIFFICULTY +++

PATHS *Good paths and tracks plus open pasture, no stiles*

LANDSCAPE *Woodland, fields and moorland fringe*

SUGGESTED MAP *OS Explorer OL21 South Pennines*

START/FINISH *Grid reference: SD 987293*

DOG FRIENDLINESS *Plenty of opportunities for dogs to be off lead*

PARKING *National Trust pay-and-display car parks at Midgehole, near Hebden Bridge (accessible via A6033, Keighley Road)*

PUBLIC TOILETS *At Gibson Mill during opening hours*

Hebden Bridge, just 4 miles (6.4km) from the Yorkshire/Lancashire border, has been a popular place to visit ever since the railway was extended across the Pennines, through the Calder Valley. But those train passengers weren't coming for a day out in a grimy little mill town; the big attraction was the wooded valley of Hebden Dale – usually called 'Hardcastle Crags' – just a short charabanc ride away. 'Hebden Bridge for Hardcastle Crags' was the stationmaster's cry, as trains approached the station. Here were shady woods, easy riverside walks and places to spread out a picnic blanket. To people who lived in the terraced streets of Bradford, Leeds or Halifax, Hardcastle Crags must have seemed idyllic. The steep-sided valley reminded Swiss visitors of their own country, and became 'Little Switzerland' – at least to the writers of tourist brochures. The only disappointment, in fact, was the crags themselves: unassuming gritstone outcrops, almost hidden by trees.

Industrial Demands

The Industrial Revolution created a huge demand for water: for mills, factories and domestic use. To quench the thirst of the rapidly expanding textile towns, many steep-sided valleys, known in the South Pennines as cloughs, were dammed to create reservoirs. Six of these lie within easy walking distance of Hardcastle Crags. They represented huge feats of civil engineering by the hundreds of navvies who built them, around the end of the 19th century, with picks and shovels. The men were housed in a shanty town, known as Dawson City and both men and materials were transported to the work-sites by a convoluted steam-powered railway system that crossed the valley on an elaborate wooden viaduct.

Hardcastle Crags escaped the indignity of being turned into a reservoir, but it was touch and go. Three times during the last 50 years (the last time was in 1970) plans were drawn up to flood the valley. And three times, thankfully, wiser counsels prevailed and the plans were turned down. Lord Savile, a major landowner in the area, once owned the valley. It was he who supplemented the natural woodland with plantings of new trees – particularly pines, and laid out the walks and the carriage drive. In 1948 Lord Savile donated Hardcastle Crags, and the nearby valley of Crimsworth Dean, to the National Trust. Because of this bequeathment, the future of this delightful valley looks secure and local people will continue to enjoy this valuable amenity.

Hardcastle Crags are a haven for wildlife. Bird watchers can look out for pied flycatchers, woodpeckers, jays, sparrowhawks and the ubiquitous dipper – which never strays from the environs of Hebden Water. In spring there are displays of bluebells; in summer the woods are filled with bird-song; the beech woods are a riot of colour as the leaves turn each autumn.

WALK 49 DIRECTIONS

❶ From the non-member pay-and-display car park, walk back to the main drive. Go left towards the lodge but, just past the information board, immediately double back right on a path falling to a picnic area beside the river. Keep left whenever there is a choice of paths and continue upstream for 1 mile (1.6km) to Gibson Mill, occasionally climbing above the river where it becomes constricted between rocky banks.

❷ Joining the main drive, follow it beyond the mill, soon passing the crags that give the woods their name. Keep right at a later fork,

WHILE YOU'RE THERE

Walk the old road from Hebden Bridge to Haworth (it's marked as such on the OS map) that includes the section of track through wooded Crimsworth Dean. The old road is never hard to find, and offers easy walking with terrific views all the way. Have lunch in Haworth, and take the easy way back to Hebden Bridge – by bus.

shortly emerging from the trees and the National Trust estate to join a rough metalled drive. It runs left to the farm and adjacent cottages at Walshaw, which enjoy a terrific prospect along the Hebden Water valley.

❸ Just before you reach the houses – when you are opposite some barns – turn sharp right through a gate on to an enclosed track (signed to Crimsworth Dean). Running on as a field track, it peters out beyond another gate to follow a wall over the shoulder of Shackleton Knoll. Approaching the watershed, the path slips through a gate to continue on the wall's opposite flank. Developing as a track, it later turns through another gate and drops into Crimsworth Dean, ending at a junction beside the ruin of Nook

Farm. Running the length of the valley, the rough way is the old road from Hebden Bridge to Haworth and is a great walk to contemplate for another day.

❹ For now, however, turn right along this elevated track, passing a farm on the left. You can make a short detour right at the next fork to see Abel Cross, actually a pair of old waymarker stones standing beside the track. Return to the main track and continue down the valley, soon re-entering the woodland of the National Trust estate. Keep left at successive forks, eventually returning to the car parks at Midgehole.

WHAT TO LOOK OUT FOR

Hebden Water rushes attractively through the wooded valley of Hardcastle Crags. These upland rivers and streams are the perfect habitat for an attractive little bird called the dipper. Dark brown, with a blaze of white on the breast, the dipper never strays from water. Unique among British birds, it has perfected the trick of walking underwater.

WHERE TO EAT AND DRINK

The Pack Horse Inn can be found on the unclassified road between Colden and Brierfield, just beyond the wooded valley of Hardcastle Crags. The Packhorse is one of many solitary, exposed pubs to be found in Pennine Yorkshire, which existed to cater for the drovers and packhorse men. There's a warm welcome for walkers, and hearty meals. In winter, though, the pub only opens at lunchtimes at the weekend.

Halifax and the Shibden Valley

An old packhorse track, a superb half-timbered hall and a hidden valley — all just a short walk from Halifax.

DISTANCE *5 miles (8km)* MINIMUM TIME *2hrs 30min*

ASCENT/GRADIENT *1,148ft (350m)* ▲▲▲ LEVEL OF DIFFICULTY ✚✚✚

PATHS *Old packhorse tracks and field paths, no stiles*

LANDSCAPE *Surprisingly rural, considering the proximity to Halifax*

SUGGESTED MAP *OS Explorer 288 Bradford & Huddersfield*

START/FINISH *Grid reference: SE 096251*

DOG FRIENDLINESS *Keep on lead crossing busy roads*

PARKING *In Halifax*

PUBLIC TOILETS *Halifax bus station and Shibden Park*

Set amongst the Pennine hills, Halifax was a town in the vanguard of the Industrial Revolution. Its splendid civic buildings and huge mills are a good indication of the town's prosperity, won from the woollen trade. Ironically, the most splendid building of all came close to being demolished. The Piece Hall, built in 1779, predates the industrial era. Here, in a total of 315 rooms on three colonnaded floors, the hand-weavers of the district would offer their wares (known as 'pieces') for sale to cloth merchants. The colonnades surround a massive square. Your first reaction on walking into the square may be surprise, for this is a building that would not look out of place in Renaissance Italy.

The mechanisation of the weaving process left the Piece Hall largely redundant. In the intervening years it has served a variety of purposes, including as a venue for political oration and as a wholesale market. During the 1970s, having narrowly escaped the wrecking ball, the Piece Hall was spruced up and given a new lease of life. It now houses a visitor centre, art gallery and speciality shops and hosts a programme of events throughout the year.

The Magna Via

The cobbled thoroughfare that climbs so steeply up Beacon Hill is known as the Magna Via. Until 1741, when a turnpike road was built, this was the only practicable approach to Halifax from the east, for both foot and packhorse traffic. Also known as Wakefield Gate, the Magna Via linked up with the Long Causeway, the old high level road to Burnley. That intrepid 18th-century traveller, Daniel Defoe, was one of those who struggled up this hill. 'We quitted Halifax not without some astonishment at its situation, being so surrounded with hills, and those so high as makes the coming in and going out of it exceedingly troublesome'. The route was superseded in the 1820s by the turnpike constructed through Godley Cutting. Today the Magna Via, too steep to be adopted for modern motor vehicles, remains a fascinating relic of the past.

Shibden Hall

Situated on a hill above Halifax, this magnificent half-timbered house is set in 90 acres (36ha) of rolling parkland. Dating from 1420, the hall has been owned by prominent local families – the Oates, Saviles, Waterhouses and, latterly, the Listers. All these families left their mark on the fabric of the house, but the core of the original house remains intact. The rooms are furnished in period style, to show how they might have looked over almost six centuries. The oak furniture and panelling has that patina of age that antique forgers try in vain to emulate. Barns and other outbuildings have been converted into a folk museum, with displays of old vehicles, tools and farm machinery.

When Emily Brontë created Thrushcross Grange in her only novel *Wuthering Heights*, she may have had Shibden Hall in mind. It certainly proved a suitable location in 1991 for a new film version of the famous story, which starred Ralph Fiennes as Heathcliffe and Juliette Binoche as Cathy.

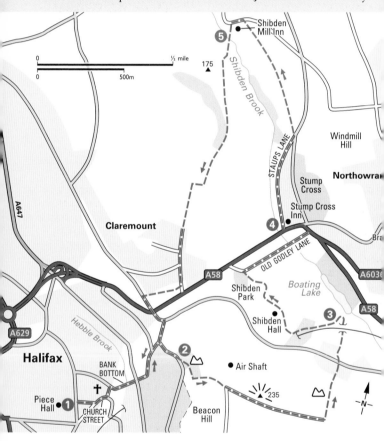

WALK 50 DIRECTIONS

❶ Begin opposite the tall spire that once belonged to Square Church, walking down Alfred Street and left along Church Street, passing the smoke-blackened parish church. Bear left again into Lower Kirkgate, then right along Bank Bottom. Cross Hebble Brook and walk uphill; where the road bears sharp left, keep straight ahead up a steep cobbled lane. When you meet a

HALIFAX

road, go right for about 200yds (183m). Just after the entrance to a warehouse (Aquaspersion), take a cobbled path on the left that makes a steep ascent up Beacon Hill.

2 This old packhorse track – known as the Magna Via – joins another path and continues uphill to a large retaining wall, where you have a choice of tracks. Keep left on a cinder track, slightly downhill, as views open up of the surprisingly rural Shibden Valley. Keep left when the track forks again; after a further 100yds (91m) take a walled path on the left. Drop steeply to a small housing estate, passing through to the main road. Almost opposite, beside a farm entrance, a path continues downhill, passing beneath the railway line into Shibden Park.

3 Walk through to the boating lake and bear left at a sign to Shibden Hall. At the next signpost, keep left again above a children's play area to follow a track beside

the railway embankment. To visit the hall, gardens and displays, go left by a pond – otherwise, take the other path signed to the car park and facilities. At the next junction, go right past a display of traditional walling, descending through trees to a drive. Climb to the gates and turn right down Old Godley Lane, which ultimately swings left up to the main road at Stump Cross.

4 Cross over the road and take Staups Lane, to the left of the Stump Cross Inn. Walk along the lane, which soon becomes cobbled, to meet another road at the top. Go left and immediately left again down a track, which, through a gate, continues across the fields into Shibden Dale. Emerging at the far end onto a lane, turn left down to the Shibden Mill Inn.

5 Swing past the pub to the far end of its car park, where a track crosses Shibden Beck. Later, bear right at a fork and continue to an isolated house. Beyond, the track narrows to a walled path. Reaching the houses of Claremount, keep ahead along a street that then bends right above Godley Cutting to a bridge spanning the A58. Over that, a flight of steps on the right drops down to the street below. Go left to its end and retrace your outward route back into Halifax.

Walking in Safety

All these walks are suitable for any reasonably fit person, but less experienced walkers should try the easier walks first. Route finding is usually straightforward, but you will find that an Ordnance Survey map is a useful addition to the route maps and descriptions.

RISKS

Although each walk here has been researched with a view to minimising the risks to the walkers who follow its route, no walk in the countryside can be considered to be completely free from risk. Walking in the outdoors will always require a degree of common sense and judgement to ensure that it is as safe as possible.

- Be particularly careful on cliff paths and in upland terrain, where the consequences of a slip can be very serious.

- Remember to check tidal conditions before walking on the seashore.

- Some sections of route are by, or cross, busy roads. Take care and remember traffic is a danger even on minor country lanes.

- Be careful around farmyard machinery and livestock, especially if you have children with you.

- Be aware of the consequences of changes in the weather and check the forecast before you set out. Carry spare clothing and a torch if you are walking in the winter months. Remember the weather can change very quickly at any time of the year, and in moorland and heathland areas, mist and fog can make route finding much harder. Don't set out in these conditions unless you are confident of your navigation skills in poor visibility. In summer remember to take account of the heat and sun; wear a hat and carry spare water.

- On walks away from centres of population you should carry a whistle and survival bag. If you do have an accident requiring the emergency services, make a note of your position as accurately as possible and dial 999.

COUNTRYSIDE CODE

- Be safe, plan ahead and follow any signs.

- Leave gates and property as you find them.

- Protect plants and animals and take your litter home.

- Keep dogs under close control.

- Consider other people.

For more information visit www.countrysideaccess.gov.uk/things_to_know/countryside_code